Stress-Free Sewing

Troubleshooting Tips and Advice
for the Savvy Sewer

SEARCH PRESS

A RotoVision book

Published in 2013 by Search Press Ltd.
Wellwood, North Farm Road
Tunbridge Wells
Kent, TN2 3DR

This book is produced by
RotoVision SA
Sheridan House, 114 Western Road
Hove
BN3 1DD

ISBN: 9781844487981

Commissioning Editor: Isheeta Mustafi
Editor: Cath Senker
Art Director: Emily Portnoi
Art Editor: Jennifer Osborne
Design and layout: Rebecca Stephenson
Photography: Sherry Heck
Stylist: Heather Sansky
Additional photography: Dana Willard
Illustrations: Rob Brandt and Lucy Smith
Cover Design: Emily Portnoi
Patterns on pages 90–93 reproduced courtesy of Simplicity

Printed in China by 1010 Printing International Ltd.

Stress-Free Sewing

Troubleshooting Tips and Advice for the Savvy Sewer

NICOLE VASBINDER

Contents

SECTION TWO
Solutions and Tips   72

How to use this book

I started teaching sewing classes in 2003 and since then I have taught thousands of people from all walks of life how to sew. During this time, the same questions have come up over and over. What sort of sewing machine should I buy? Do I need a serger? How do I make this pattern fit? What tools do I really need? My goal in all of my sewing classes is to make sewing fun and non-stressful. I really believe that sewing is a life skill that can bring you so much joy and fulfilment. Although it may cost you more money upfront to make something than to simply buy it in a shop, you can get exactly what you want in the colours and fabrics you love. You'll be able to make it fit correctly and use better-quality construction techniques so it doesn't fall apart in the wash. And you will take better care of something if you have put the time, money and energy into making it. Trust me, if you get a stain on your homemade skirt, you will get that stain out! So, instead of having a gigantic closet full of nothing to wear, you can have a smaller wardrobe where everything is special, well made and you love and wear every piece. Ultimately, that can save you money.

I find that many people don't understand how their sewing machine works and do not realise that all sewing machines operate and thread the same way. I will show you how to troubleshoot common machine issues so that you can quickly solve the problem and get on with your project. I'll explain all the basic and not so basic sewing tools; notions, fabrics, and trims; how to use them and where you can buy them. I'll explain where you can substitute a common household item for a specialist tool and go over both basic and complex sewing techniques. This book takes the worry and frustration out of sewing and offers invaluable advice you can trust, at your fingertips.

ICON KEY

Buying and choosing   Working with   Technique   Best practice   Health and safety

I have really intended for this book to be the essential reference book for the new generation of sewers and sewers of all abilities. Organised by the stages in a project, from choosing tools and materials, through reading and understanding patterns to fitting and adding embellishments and closures, all the information is presented so you know exactly where to look when you get stuck with a problem. Illustrated entries cover every aspect and item in the sewing process, with each entry providing the characteristics, pros and cons and basic considerations of working with that item. Icons on each page tell you whether tips relate to buying and choosing materials; using and working with them; techniques and tutorials; or safety considerations (see Icon Key table above). Cross-references take you between chapters so you can see how different aspects relate to each other, and there are clever tips on how to deal with virtually any sewing situation.

I sincerely hope that this book becomes an indispensable part of your library and pushes you to a new level of creativity and confidence. Happy sewing!

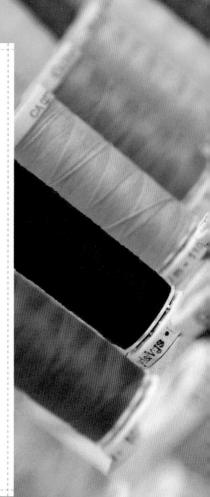

SECTION ONE
Tools and Equipment

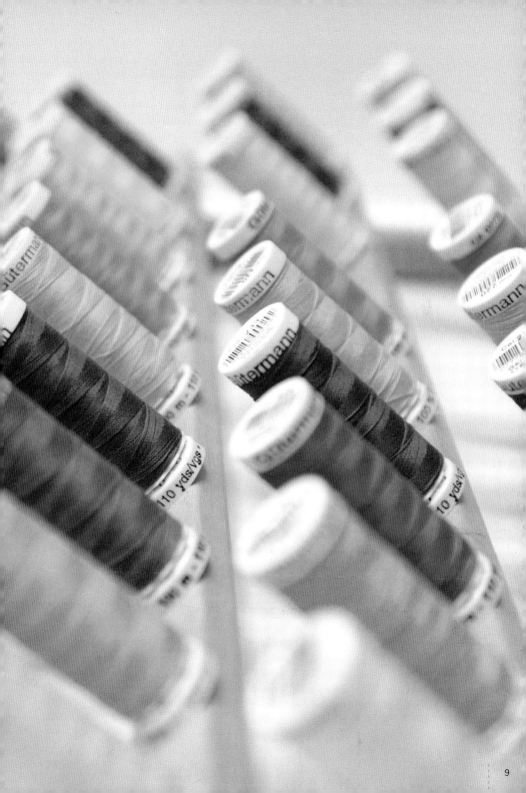

SELECTOR

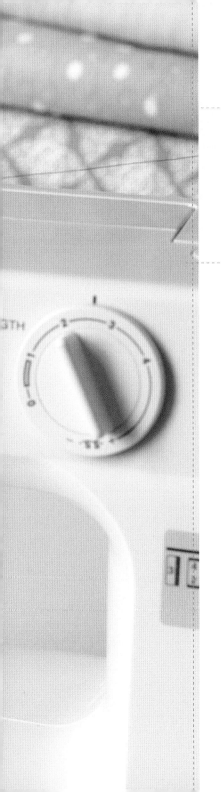

CHAPTER 1
SEWING TOOLS

The right tools make any job easier and that's true in sewing as well. But the choices available in the marketplace can be overwhelming. Do you need everything? Do you have to spend a lot of money? Learn what is essential and what can be a helpful optional feature.

The basic sewing machine

The sewing machine is the biggest financial investment for sewers and choosing the right one for you is important – you will have it for years and use it for nearly every sewing project. There are so many different brands available at many different price points, and making a choice can be overwhelming. One thing to keep in mind is that, at heart, all sewing machines do the same basic thing. They all use an upper thread and a lower thread to create a lockstitch and connect one piece of fabric to another. They all have the same basic parts. All sewing machines have a spool pin to hold the upper thread; thread guides; tension discs; take-up lever; a needle; feed dog; presser foot; bobbin and bobbin case for the lower thread; controls to adjust stitch pattern, length, and width; a bobbin winder, and a foot pedal. It doesn't matter how old the machine is or what brand it is; the basic design of a sewing machine really hasn't changed in a hundred years.

Types of sewing machines

Simple mechanical sewing machines can do all the basic utility stitches. There are also fancy computerised sewing machines that automatically adjust settings for different stitches and have lots of decorative embroidery stitches. And there are super-fancy embroidery sewing machines that can be hooked up to your computer so you can download embroidery and stitch patterns from the Internet. Note that sewing machines are designed with either a front-load bobbin or a top-load bobbin. You can buy a brand-new machine or a used, refurbished or vintage machine. Some of my favourite machines are older models that may not be swanky, but are built like tanks from metal parts and will last forever.

Top: *Basic sewing machine*
Middle: *Machine with a front-load bobbin*
Bottom: *Machine with a top-load bobbin*

Where to get your machine

You can buy a sewing machine from a specialist dealer, from a chain store, online, at charity shops and car-boot sales. Ask friends who sew what they like and dislike about their sewing machines. I always recommend that you buy a sewing machine from a store where you can test it out first. While all sewing machines can do the same basic things, some machines are fast and some are slow. Some are loud and some are quiet, and you won't know until you sew on it. Think of it like buying a car. You would take it for a test drive before buying, right? Also, many sewing machine dealers offer free lessons with the purchase of your machine and may also offer trade-ins if you want to upgrade in the future. If you do buy online or from a chain store, make sure it has a generous return policy in case you don't like the machine.

Every sewer should know

You should look for a quality machine that is made from as many metal parts as possible. While plastic parts and construction make for a lightweight machine that is easy to carry around, unfortunately, this type tends not to last as long as a machine of all-metal construction. Will you be able to hem jeans on it? You want a machine with a strong motor that can sew through many layers of thick fabric. How does it sew on thin knits? You also want a model that has enough finesse to handle more delicate fabrics. Does it have a sensitive foot pedal or a speed control? This can very helpful for beginners because they tend to be a bit heavy footed and sew too fast.

Which accessories and feet are included with the machine? Will you end up spending lots of money on accessories that were not included? If the feet and accessories are not included, are they readily available? Can you use generic feet or only brand-specific feet? The most commonly used feet are the zigzag, zipper, buttonhole, button, and overcast.

SEE ALSO

page 18: Presser feet

Q. HOW OFTEN SHOULD I CLEAN MY MACHINE AND WHAT HAPPENS IF I DON'T?

A. You should definitely clean your machine every couple of weeks. Thread sheds as it moves through the upper threading path and needle and leaves lint behind. As the needle punctures the fabric, that also creates lint in the bobbin mechanism and under the feed dog. If you don't clean your machine, then the lint will build up, get packed into the moving parts and stop them from moving. Your machine should come with a little brush (or you can purchase one at any fabric store), which you should use to brush out the lint from the feed dog, bobbin area and threading path.

BOBBINS

You should also know which type of bobbin your machine takes. The two most common types of bobbins are the Class 15 bobbin and Class 66. Both are available in plastic or metal. Class 15 is the one most machines use, whether front load or top load. The Class 66 tends to fit Singer drop-in machines but not all. Yet there are many other types of bobbins specific to different machines. There are special bobbins for Singer Futura, Touch & Sew and Featherweight machines. Some Elna machines use a specific bobbin as well as some Vikings. Always check your manual because using the wrong bobbin can cause threads to jam and may damage your machine. See page 102 for information on winding bobbins.

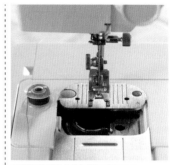

Top: *Top-load bobbin case with a Class 66 plastic bobbin*
Bottom: *Front-load bobbin case with a Class 15 metal bobbin*

TIPS

Top-load bobbins should always load into the bobbin case in the shape of a letter P, with the thread pulling off the bobbin from the top to the left.

Front-load bobbins should always load into the bobbin case in the shape of a number 9, with the thread pulling off the bobbin from the top to the right.

STITCHES

While some of the higher-end computerised machines can do a seemingly endless amount of stitches, I find that there are really only a few that are absolutely necessary and everything else is optional. The most important stitch is the straight stitch and you will use that for about 99 percent of all your sewing. It is the basic construction stitch that connects one piece of fabric to another. Next up is the zigzag stitch. You can use this for appliqué, topstitch, finishing seam allowances, sewing on buttons, monograms, embroidery, stretch fabrics and more. An easy-to-use buttonhole stitch is important if you're going to make clothes. You might also want a blind hem stitch if you are going to make clothes or are planning on doing a lot of hemming. The other stitches tend to be seam finishes, decorative or more advanced stitches for knits, and are a bonus!

SEE ALSO

page 102: *Machine basics*

Top: *Stitch selection on a computerised sewing machine*
Bottom: *Correct upper threading*

Q. WHY ARE MY THREADS JAMMING?

A. The key to trouble-free sewing is to thread the machine correctly. All sewing machines thread the same way on the top. While things might look a little different and be in slightly different places, it's always the same sequence of steps (see page 104). Missing a step or changing the order of steps will definitely cause thread jams, tangles and problems.

The serger/overlock machine

Sergers (also known as overlockers or overlock machines) came on the home market in the 1960s. They make a multiple-thread chain stitch and can stitch, trim and overcast the seam allowance in a single operation. They can be used for seaming, hemming and edging. Sergers are also extremely useful for sewing knits and stretch fabrics because the chain stitch can stretch. They operate much faster than regular sewing machines and can create very professional results. However, they do not replace your regular machine because they cannot be used to install zips and cannot stitch buttonholes. Instead, they complement a standard sewing machine.

Types of sergers

Sergers are commonly available with two, three, four and five thread capabilities. Instead of a bobbin, sergers have loopers that pull threads directly from spools. They also have a stitch finger that the chain forms over. They will have two to three loopers and one to two needles to create the overlock chainstitch. Different types of stitches will be created depending on how many needles and which loopers are used.

Other features

A serger also has knives that trim the seam allowances and stray threads just before the fabric passes under the needles. Just like standard sewing machines, sergers have a feed dog to move the fabric through the machine. But many sergers also have a feature called differential feed, which is a second feed dog that can move at a different speed to either create gathers or prevent fabric from rippling. They also have settings so that you can adjust the stitch length, width and tensions. The most common type of serger is a 3/4-thread model that uses two loopers and one or two needles. The five-thread serger gives the most options and some five-thread models can also stitch a coverstitch.

Top: A standard 3/4-thread serger threaded for three-thread overcasting
Middle: Serger loopers and knives
Bottom: A three-thread overlock on the left, a coverstitch on the right

Where to buy one

You can purchase a serger anywhere you can buy a standard sewing machine: at sewing machine dealerships, chain stores and online. Sergers tend to be pricier than sewing machines. As with regular machines, I would recommend buying from a dealer so that you can test the machine in the store and make sure that you understand how to thread it correctly and change all the different settings.

Every sewer should know

The threading sequence on a serger is crucial to successfully operating the machine. Threading the different threads out of order will cause the thread to jam, break or become unthreaded, or the machine won't be able to create the chain. Always make sure that you consult the manual to thread the serger correctly.

You should be able to disengage the knives by either turning a knob or removing them. This is necessary when doing a rolled hem or coverstitch. You should also be able to disengage the stitch finger for different functions such as a rolled hem or blind hem.

Because the serger is fast and creates a chain stitch, it uses a lot of thread, so you will need to buy large spools of thread. However, the loopers use up the thread more quickly than the needles, so you should either rotate the threads periodically or buy larger spools for the loopers. You can also use speciality threads in the loopers, such as embroidery threads, to create beautiful effects.

SEE ALSO
page 28: Threads

Q. DO I NEED TO RETHREAD THE SERGER EVERY TIME I CHANGE COLOURS?

A. No! You can change colours by tying on new threads. Cut off the old threads at the spools. Remove the old spools and replace with the new ones and tie the new threads on to the old threads. Pull the threads through until the new colours are threaded. You will need to manually rethread the needles because the knots will be too large to pull through the needle eyes, but they will easily pull through the loopers. The tie-on method is also very helpful for getting larger novelty threads through the loopers.

Q. DO I BACKSTITCH ON A SERGER?

A. No, sergers do not stitch in reverse. To secure the stitches, you chain off and can either tie the chain in a knot, use a tapestry or yarn needle to pull the threads back through the chain or use a drop of seam sealant to secure the threads.

Presser feet

The various presser feet available can make sewing tasks much faster and easier. Some come as standard with a sewing machine and others have to be purchased separately.

Snap-on and screw-on feet

Some machines have snap-on feet and others use screw-on feet. To change screw-on feet, remove the shank from your machine. Snap-on feet have a release lever or button on the back. The shank stays on the machine and you can quickly change feet. If your machine is designed for only screw-on feet, you can get a snap-foot shank so you can use feet that come only in the snap-on option.

BASIC FEET

The zigzag foot is an all-purpose foot with a wide slot to allow the needle to move back and forth. The straight-stitch foot has a small hole and is used only for straight stitching with the needle in the centre position. It prevents the needle from pushing fabric down into the needle hole and can help with straight and accurate topstitching. The zigzag foot comes as standard. The straight-stitch foot needs to be purchased separately for lower-priced machines.

┌─────────────┐
╎ **SEE ALSO** ╎·
└─────────────┘
page 112: *Basic stitches*
page 134: *Sewing on trims*

Top: *L to R*: *low shank, high shank, slant shank*
Middle: *L to R*: *screw-on low shank foot, snap-on low shank foot*
Bottom: *L to R*: *straight-stitch foot, zigzag foot*

ZIPPER FEET

Standard zipper feet are narrow to allow the needle to stitch close to the zip teeth. They can be positioned to either the left or right of the zip and can be used on all types of zips. Standard zipper feet can also be used for stitching on piping and welting if you do not have a piping or welting foot. The invisible zipper foot is used only on invisible zips and has channels into which the zip coils fit. This will allow you to stitch very close to the zip coil. A standard zipper foot comes with most machines while an invisible zipper foot comes as standard only with high-end machines.

SEE ALSO

page 47: Zips
page 38: Piping
page 132: Piping and welting
page 182: Zips

BUTTONHOLE AND BUTTON FEET

A buttonhole foot has a sliding window and markings to help you see and size your buttonholes. There are grooves on the bottom to ride over the raised stitches of a buttonhole to help keep the stitching even. Button feet have short toes that are usually coated to hold a sew-through button in place while you use a zigzag stitch to sew the button on. You can also use a button foot to stitch on rings and some trims. A buttonhole foot comes standard on most machines. A button foot will be included on higher-end machines.

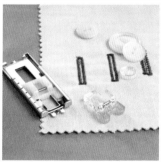

Top: *L to R*: screw-on invisible zipper foot, snap-on standard zipper foot, screw-on standard zipper foot
Bottom: *L to R*: snap-on manual buttonhole foot, snap-on button foot

SEE ALSO

page 42: Buttons
page 170: Buttons and buttonholes
page 112: Basic stitches
page 134: Sewing on trims
page 179: Buckles
page 180: D-rings and O-rings

TIP

Some sewing machines use low shank feet, some use high shank and some use slant shank. Most home machines use low shank, but make sure that you are using the correct type for your machine.

HEM FEET

Hem feet allow you to achieve professional hems far more quickly than with an all-purpose foot. The rolled hem foot is used to turn a narrow amount of fabric over twice and stitch it down in one smooth motion. The blind hem foot creates an invisible hem where you don't want to see visible topstitching on the right side. Both types are standard on all but the most basic machines.

page 112: *Basic stitches*
page 162: *Hems*

SEAM FINISHING FEET

An overcast foot has a little stitch finger or prong to hold down the raw edges of a seam allowance while you use a seam finish stitch such as a zigzag stitch or overcast. The prong prevents the edges from bunching up. The stitch in the ditch foot has a centre bar that rides in an existing seam to allow you to accurately stitch down the centre; this foot is often used for edgestitching and topstitching. An overcast foot comes standard on all but the most basic machines, while the stitch in the ditch foot is usually standard only on high-end machines.

page 108: *Seam allowance*

Top: *L to R: snap-on rolled hem foot, snap-on blind hem foot*
Bottom: *L to R: snap-on overcast foot, snap-on stitch in the ditch foot*

EMBROIDERY AND QUILTING FEET

The satin-stitch foot has a little groove on the bottom to allow for the buildup of stitches when doing satin stitches, monogramming and appliqué. It can be used for all types of decorative stitches. The foot is usually clear to give you a good view. Many people use this as an all-purpose foot.

The 6mm (¼in) foot is well named because it has a 6mm right toe and a fabric guide that is incredibly helpful for quilters who need precise measurements. This foot can also be used for topstitching.

The appliqué foot is similar to the satin-stitch foot but it is completely clear with a short open toe for even better visibility.

The free-motion embroidery foot is also known as a darning foot. The spring and hook that sit over the needle bar work in place of the feed dog as your hands move the fabric around. The open toe allows for excellent visibility while you are stitching.

The even-feed foot is also known as a walking foot. It has its own feed dog to allow both layers of fabric to move evenly and together. Frequently sold with an adjustable quilt bar, it is perfect for maintaining accuracy on many layers of fabric but also when seaming plaids and stripes.

Only the satin-stitch foot is standard with most machines. The 6mm foot and even-feed foot may be standard on machines marketed to quilters, but if yours did not come with one, it is readily available. The appliqué foot and free-motion embroidery foot are usually optional on all but the highest-end machines.

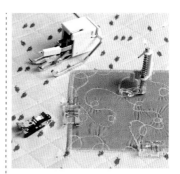

Top: *Front row L to R: snap-on 6mm foot, snap-on satin-stitch foot, snap-on appliqué foot*
Back row L to R: screw-on even feed/walking foot with quilt bar, screw-on free-motion embroidery foot

Q. DO I NEED ALL THESE FEET?

A. No, you can achieve many of these sewing techniques with an all-purpose foot but these feet can make your work faster and easier and allow you to do some high-end sewing on even the most basic machines.

SEE ALSO

page 112: Basic stitches
page 108: Stitching basics
page 138: Fabric appliqué

Handsewing needles

While most of your sewing will be by machine, there are certain times that handsewing is faster or preferable. Handsewing needles are made of metal and have an eye at the end.

Types of hand needles

The size, length, point and eye size allow for different tasks and work on different fabrics and with different types of thread. Needles are sized by number, with large needles having low numbers and fine needles having high numbers.

Most commonly used

Sharps are an all-purpose medium-length needle with a sharp point. Betweens are shorter than sharps and are used for detail work. Darners are longer and are used for mending and darning holes. Embroidery needles have a longer eye than sharps to accommodate multiple strands of embroidery floss. Tapestry needles have a large eye and blunt point and are used for needlepoint and decorative stitching. The blunt tip goes through fabric without creating a hole. Chenille needles have a large eye for yarn or ribbon and a sharp point for decorative stitching. Beading needles are very long, thin and flexible and are used to stitch beads and sequins on to fabric. Yarn darners are similar to tapestry needles but are even bigger and with a larger eye and are sometimes made of plastic.

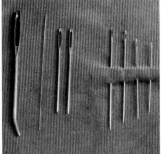

Top: *A standard book of assorted needles*
Middle: *L to R: yarn darner, beading, tapestry, chenille, embroidery, darner, between, sharp needle*
Bottom: *L to R: canvas, carpet, leather, sacks, sail, small upholstery, large upholstery needle*

There are also speciality needles that are frequently found in a booklet called repair needles. Canvas and carpet needles are similar to sharps, but are heavier for going through thick materials. Leather needles have a triangular point that easily passes through the material without damaging it. Sack needles are similar to tapestry needles, but are bigger for loosely woven fabric. Sail needles are like large leather needles for working on heavy sailcloth and other heavy fabrics. Curved upholstery needles allow you to get into hard-to-reach areas.

Where to get them
You can purchase handsewing needles at any craft or fabric store.

Every sewer should know
You can buy a book of assorted needles or a package of one type of needle.

┌─ **SEE ALSO** ┐

page 112: *Basic stitches*
page 134: *Sewing on trims*

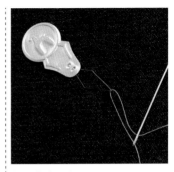

A needle threader in use

Q. **IS THERE AN EASY WAY TO THREAD A NEEDLE?**

A. Yes. Needle threaders are little wire loops on a handle. They easily glide through even the smallest needle eyes and then you drop your thread through the large loop and pull it back through the eye of the needle. Needle threaders often come with a book of needles or you can purchase them separately.

Machine needles

A sewing-machine needle connects the top thread on the machine to the bobbin thread to form stitches. Household machine needles have a flat shank on the back, while needles for industrial machines have a completely round shank. On the back of the needle down near the eye is the scarf, which is an indentation that allows the top thread to pick up the bobbin thread. You must use a household needle for a standard home machine. Household needles should be marked on the package as system 130/705 H or 15x1 H. Before purchasing needles, check whether your machine requires a particular brand of needle or whether any brand will be fine.

Sizes of machine needles

Just like handsewing needles, there are many types of machine needles designed for different tasks and fabrics. They each have different-sized eyes, points and scarves. The needle package should be marked with the type of needle and the needle sizes. For machine needles, low numbers equal fine needles while high numbers mean heavy needles. The goal is to have the needle make a small hole while not breaking. There are always two numbers to indicate size. Needles are sized from 60/8 to 120/19. The first number is in the European system and the second number is in the American system. The European number is a measurement of the diameter of the needle shaft, while the American number is arbitrary.

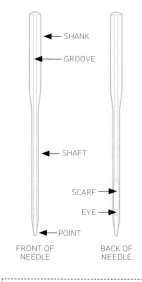

SHANK
GROOVE
SHAFT
SCARF
EYE
POINT

FRONT OF
NEEDLE

BACK OF
NEEDLE

SEWING-MACHINE NEEDLE SIZES		
AMERICAN		**EUROPEAN**
8	Lightest	60
9		65
10		70
11		75
12		80
14		90
16		100
18		110
19	Heaviest	120

Types of machine needles

- Universals are all-purpose needles that work well for most fabric types; sizes 11 and 12 are the most common.
- Jersey needles are ballpoint needles for sewing on knits without creating holes and runs.
- Stretch needles are designed for knits with lots of spandex and prevent skipped stitches.
- Leather needles have a special cutting point and help cut the hole for leather, vinyl and oilcloth.
- Denim needles have a strong shaft and sharp point for sewing through heavy fabrics without breaking.
- Microtex sharp needles have a very thin and sharp point for working with delicate fabrics and are great for perfectly straight and precise stitches.
- Embroidery, topstitch and metallic needles have large eyes for working with special threads.
- Twin needles have two needles attached to a single shaft.

Where to get them

You can purchase needles at any fabric store.

Every sewer should know

You can get a package of assorted needles that includes a variety of sizes or you can buy a package that includes all one size for the most common needles such as Universal, Jersey and Denim.

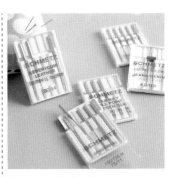

Machine needles L to R: leather, universal, jersey/ballpoint, stretch, twin jeans

Q. HOW OFTEN SHOULD I CHANGE MY NEEDLE?

A. It's a good idea to change out for a new needle every three or four projects or eight hours of sewing time. Every time the needle makes a stitch, it penetrates multiple layers of fabric and dulls a little bit. A dull needle causes skipped stitches, can damage your fabric, is prone to breaking and can cause thread jams.

CHAPTER 2
NOTIONS AND TRIMS

Once you have the basic sewing machine and
accessories, then it's time to learn about notions.
Notions refer to all sewing materials except for
fabric. They include thread, trims, buttons, zips
and more!

Threads

ALL-PURPOSE SEWING THREAD

All-purpose sewing thread is a general-use sewing thread for both machine and handsewing.

Most commonly used for

All-purpose thread is mostly used for basic seams but can also be used to stitch buttonholes, sew on trims and zips, stitch on buttons, for basting, topstitching and for free-motion embroidery.

Types of all-purpose thread

All-purpose thread comes in all the colours of the rainbow and is available in 100-percent polyester, 100-percent cotton and cotton-wrapped polyester. One-hundred percent polyester is the strongest and has a tiny amount of stretch to it. It also resists shrinkage. It is an excellent choice for most types of fabric. I use 100-percent cotton thread for sewing on silks and fine cottons such as voile and lawn. Cotton is a natural fibre, so the stitches will press flat into the fabric with the heat of an iron. However, it will be more susceptible than artificial fibres to eventual deterioration due to age, washing and exposure to sunlight and detergents. Projects made from fine fabrics such as silk will not endure lots of wear and tear, so this will not be a big concern. Since 100-percent cotton thread does not stretch, it should not be used for sewing knits or stretch fabrics. Cotton-wrapped polyester thread should be avoided.

Where to get it

You can buy thread at any fabric store.

Every sewer should know

When choosing thread colour, always pull a single strand of thread and lay it on your fabric. Squint your eyes and choose the colour that disappears. If you are debating between two colours, always go with the darker colour; it will disappear, while lighter colours tend to pop out. On the other hand, you could pick a totally contrasting colour thread.

SEE ALSO

page 122: Sewing with knits

All-purpose polyester and cotton thread

Q. HOW ARE THREADS SIZED?

A. The higher the number, the thinner and finer the thread. All-purpose thread is usually a size 50.

Q. WHY SHOULD I BUY GOOD THREAD?

A. You get what you pay for. Good thread is smooth and strong and can withstand the high speed of a sewing machine. Poor-quality thread is made from short, fuzzy fibres. It tends to break, get tangled in your machine and cause all sorts of sewing problems. Also, thread can go bad. If you have threads on wooden spools, do not use them because thread has not been made on wooden spools in about thirty years. It loses its stretch and becomes brittle over time. When in doubt, buy new thread for your project.

ELASTIC THREAD

Elastic thread is a highly stretchy thread made from a rubber core.

Types of elastic thread

Elastic thread generally comes only in black and white but you may be able to find other colours.

Most commonly used for

Elastic thread is used to create elastic shirring, which is parallel rows of straight stitching that gather up fabric and can stretch. You see this technique frequently on the bodices of sundresses, on the hems of puffed sleeves, along necklines, and at waists. It is a good technique to make a garment more fitted. The elastic thread is used in the bobbin while an all-purpose thread is used on top.

Where to get it

You can buy elastic thread at any fabric store.

Every sewer should know

You always need to hand wind the elastic thread on to the bobbin, being careful not to stretch the thread. When sewing with elastic thread, always leave long thread tails and hand tie them off. You may need to lengthen your stitch length to 3mm and definitely do a test stitch on a scrap of the same fabric you are using for your project. Also, be aware that the more rows of stitching you do, the greater the gathering effect. Finally, elastic thread can dry out and lose its stretchability so do not use old thread.

SEE ALSO
page 153: Waistline

Elastic thread used for elastic shirring

Q. MY ELASTIC SHIRRING IS NOT GATHERING.

A. Press the gathers with steam. The thread will shrink up, and gathers will appear just like magic.

SPECIALITY THREAD

Speciality threads are any type of sewing thread that is not an all-purpose sewing thread. They each serve a special purpose.

Types of speciality thread

Specialty threads include nylon upholstery thread, 100-percent polyester topstitch thread, 100-percent silk, 100-percent rayon embroidery thread and 100-percent cotton handquilting thread.

Most commonly used for

Nylon upholstery thread is very strong and thicker than all-purpose thread. It is an excellent choice for heavy-weight upholstery fabric, leather and handbags. You need to use a heavy needle such as a denim or topstitch needle when using this thread and may need to lower the upper tension slightly to accommodate the thicker thread.

Thicker than all-purpose thread, 100-percent polyester topstitch thread is frequently used in a contrasting colour on jeans. A topstitch needle is required when using this thread on the machine. Usually, you still use all-purpose thread in the bobbin and you will need to lower the upper tension to accommodate the thicker thread. It is also an excellent choice for handstitching on buttons.

One-hundred percent silk thread is very thin and strong. It works beautifully for hand basting since the smooth nature of the thread allows basting stitches to be removed easily. You can also stitch seams with it and it is a good choice for sewing on silk fabrics. You can use it for machine embroidery but this is a costly option. When machine stitching with silk thread, make sure to use a fine needle, such as a Microtex sharp needle, and tighten the tension slightly.

L to R: Polyester topstitch thread, nylon upholstery thread, rayon embroidery thread, hand-quilting thread, silk thread

Used for machine embroidery, 100-percent rayon or viscose embroidery thread is very shiny, smooth, and lustrous. It comes in solid and variegated colours. It should be used only in the upper threads while all-purpose thread is used in the bobbin. You can also try using this in the loopers on a serger. Use an embroidery needle and check your tension because it may need to be tightened.

One-hundred percent cotton hand-quilting thread is for handstitching on quilts and other handstitching projects. It has a special coating to give added strength and smoothness and prevent tangling. It is not a good choice for machine stitching because this thread is stiff and does not move through the machine well or wind on to a bobbin.

Where to get it

You can buy speciality thread at any fabric store.

Every sewer should know

Speciality threads do not come in as many colours as all-purpose threads.

SEE ALSO

page 24: Machine needles
page 138: Fabric appliqué
page 162: Hems
page 170: Buttonholes
page 174: Buttons

Q. WHAT IF I CAN'T FIND A TOPSTITCHING THREAD IN THE RIGHT COLOUR?

A. If there is the right colour in an all-purpose thread, you can use a double strand of all-purpose thread to mimic the look of heavier threads. Make sure that you use a topstitch needle because you will need the larger eye to accommodate the double thickness.

Trims

APPLIQUÉ

Appliqué refers to a technique in which a piece of fabric is sewn on to another piece of fabric. It also refers to ready-made appliqué patches.

Types of appliqué

There are hundreds of types of appliqués. They are available in very small sizes of under 2.5cm (1in) up to larger ones that can be 15cm (6in) across. Some ready-made appliqués have adhesive on the back and can be ironed on to the main fabric while others need to be stitched in place either by machine or by hand.

Most commonly used for

Appliqués can be purely decorative and can really jazz up a plain garment or item. You could design a whole project to showcase a fabulous appliqué. You can also use appliqué to cover holes and stains.

Where to get it

You can buy appliqués at any fabric store or you can make your own.

Every sewer should know

Be sure to test an iron-on appliqué after it has cooled down. Some iron-on appliqués don't stay on very well and need to be stitched down. Ready-made appliqués can be stitched down using a basic straight stitch or a satin stitch.

> SEE ALSO
>
> *page 21*: Embroidery and quilting feet
> *page 86*: Interfacing
> *page 138*: Fabric appliqué

Iron-on appliqué on top of a satin-stitched appliqué

Q. HOW DO I MAKE MY OWN APPLIQUÉS?

A. You can cut a shape out of a fabric, pin it in place and stitch across the edges using a satin stitch. A satin-stitch foot or appliqué foot makes this much easier, and applying fusible interfacing to the wrong side can keep it from stretching. You can also try pressing the raw edges under and stitching in place just in from the edge, using a straight stitch or any decorative stitch. You can also layer up appliqués for cool effects.

BEADED AND SEQUINED TRIMS

Beaded and sequined trims are any sort of sparkly decorative trim made of sequins, paillettes, beads, pearls, stones, rhinestones, crystals and jewels.

Types of beaded and sequined trims

They come in all colours and are available as fringes, strands, tapes, appliqués, and as individual beads, stones, pearls or crystals.

Most commonly used for

Beaded and sequined trims are frequently used to add a little bling to special-occasion garments and accessories but can be used anytime you want to add a little sparkle and pizzazz. Pearl trims are frequently used in bridal wear. These trims are purely decorative.

Where to get it

Good fabric stores that specialise in bridal wear should have a wide variety. You can find a good selection online.

Every sewer should know

Many beaded trims are fragile, and the garments they are used on should be dry-cleaned to protect them. Some beaded trims made with glass beads will need to be handstitched on because the presser foot can crush the beads. Others can be stitched down in place just like any ribbon or trim. For round trims like pearl and bead strand, try using a beading and piping foot and use a zigzag stitch to hold in place. Flat gems can be glued in place using fabric glue.

SEE ALSO

page 19: *Buttonhole and button feet*
page 134: *Sewing on trims*

L to R: pearl trim, beaded trim, sequin trim, loose beads

Q. HOW DO I STITCH ON SEQUIN TAPE TRIMS?

A. Use a sequin and tape foot and stitch right down the centre with a straight stitch.

Q. HOW DO I STITCH ON INDIVIDUAL BEADS AND SEQUINS?

A. Individual beads need to be handstitched and you should knot the thread every few beads just in case a thread breaks. This will prevent you from losing all the beads. Rings can be stitched down using a buttonhole foot and a zigzag stitch.

BIAS TAPE

Bias tape or bias binding is a narrow strip of fabric, cut on the bias or cross grain (see page 76) to make it more stretchable than fabric that is cut on the straight grain. It is used to make piping and binding seams, and to finish raw edges. Many strips can be pieced together to form a long tape.

Types of bias tape

Commercially available bias tape is sold as single-fold and double-fold bias tape and in different widths, with the most common being 1.3cm (1/2in) wide and 2.2cm (7/8in) wide. New bias tapes are nearly always a polyester/cotton blend but vintage bias can be found in all different fabrics, such as cotton percale and silk.

Most commonly seen on

Aside from piping, binding and finishing raw edges, bias tape is most commonly seen on edges of quilts, placemats, bibs, as dress or bag straps and around armholes and necklines.

Where to get it

Most fabric stores stock bias tape. Store-bought bias tape comes in a variety of widths and a range of solid colours, and a very limited type of patterns, such as gingham.

Every sewer should know

Homemade bias tape is great if you want a patterned bias or colour to match the fabric used in your project. It's also so simple to make that most sewers prefer to use their own rather than store bought tape!

SEE ALSO

page 66: Bias tape makers
page 76: Grainlines and bias
page 128: Bias tape

Wide and regular single-fold bias tape

Q. CAN YOU MAKE BIAS TAPE?

A. Yes, you can make it at home using bias tape makers, which come in a range of sizes.

Q. WHY USE BIAS STRIPS?

A. Most woven fabrics (unless they have a bit of spandex blended in) have no stretch. But if you tug a piece of woven fabric along the bias, the fabric will give a little bit. It's not that it 'stretches' but it has some 'ease' to it. Tape made from bias-cut fabric forms around curves much more easily, without causing fabric to pucker.

BRAIDED TRIMS

Braided trim (also known as gimp or guimp) is a type of decorative trim that comes in a range of colours, shapes and narrow widths.

Types of braided trim

Braided trims can be made of cotton, polyester, metallics, and rayon, and also blends of fibres. They are frequently shiny. Braided trims can be extremely simple and casual or formal and dressy.

Most commonly seen on

Braided trims are traditionally used on upholstery to disguise the nail heads that hold the fabric to the wooden frame of upholstered furniture, but they are also used on curtains and pillows. They can also be used on garments and accessories.

Where to get it

The chain craft and fabric stores may have a limited selection but the better fabric stores that specialise in bridal wear and fashion fabrics should have a good selection. You can also find a good variety online.

Every sewer should know

Natural fibre trims can be dyed so if you can't find a perfect colour match, try dyeing one. Make sure to use a dye formulated for the fibre content of your trim.

SEE ALSO >

page 22: Handsewing needles
page 134: Sewing on trims

Braided gimp trims

Q. HOW DO I ATTACH BRAIDED TRIMS?

A. On furniture and upholstery, braids are either glued on or handstitched. When stitching them on, you might want to try using an upholstery needle. On garments, accessories and pillows you can stitch them directly in place. Try using invisible thread to disguise the stitching.

ELASTICS

Elastic trims are flexible and stretchable narrow strips that gather up fabric to allow for ease of movement and fit. They have either a rubber or spandex core and are wrapped in cotton, polyester, nylon or other fibre. They come in widths ranging from 3mm (⅛in) up to wider widths, such as 10cm (4in).

Types of elastic trims

Elastic trims can be braided or knitted tapes that are hidden in seams or in decorative styles designed to be visible, such as foldover elastic and picot-edge elastics. Basic elastics tend to come only in black or white but fashion elastics such as picot and foldover come in many colours.

Left: Top to Bottom: 19mm (¾in) knitted non-roll elastic, 6mm (¼in) braided elastic, 1cm (⅜in) picot-edge elastic, 1.3cm (½in) braided elastic

Right: Top to Bottom: 1.3cm (½in) knit elastic, assorted picot-edge elastics

Most commonly seen on

Elastics are frequently used in casings at waistlines but also at necklines and on sleeves.

Where to get it

You can buy basic elastics either by the yard or in prepackaged lengths at any fabric store. The more decorative elastics can be harder to find. You can also find a good selection online.

Q. CAN I SEW WITH ELASTICS?

A. Yes, elastic thread can be used to sew with.

Every sewer should know

Braided elastics are used inside casings. They become narrower as they stretch and should never be stitched through because that can cause them to lose stretch. Knitted elastics don't narrow when stretched and can be stitched through, meaning they can be stitched directly on to fabric or used in casings. Always exercise your elastic before cutting and sewing by stretching it a couple of times to ensure that it returns to its original length.

Q. DOES ELASTIC SHRINK?

A. Yes, elastic can shrink in the wash and can also lose its elasticity over time, especially in the dryer.

SEE ALSO
page 29: *Elastic thread*
page 134: *Sewing on trims*
page 153: *Waistline*

LACE

Lace trims are narrow fabrics characterised by openwork and holes. They frequently have floral motifs and can add a romantic element to any design. They can be used to create an heirloom or old-fashioned look or to produce a very upscale style.

L to R: Cotton eyelet edging, polyester venise lace galloon, two-tone cotton eyelet edging

Types of lace trims

Lace trims can have a single border – these are called edgings. There are also double-border lace trims, known as galloons. Lace types include fancy venise lace, Chantilly, eyelet and crochet. While lace is usually only in white, ivory and black, you can sometimes find it in other colours. Lace trims can be made of nearly any fibre but you will most often see cotton, polyester, rayon and silk.

Most commonly seen on

Lace trimmings are very popular for bridal, lingerie, evening wear, heirloom sewing and girls' dresses. You frequently see lace as edgings at necklines, sleeves and skirt hems.

Where to get it

You can buy basic lace trims at any fabric store but you will find the biggest selection at stores that specialise in bridal and fashion fabrics. You can also find a good selection online.

Every sewer should know

You can layer lace trims with other types of trim, such as satin or grosgrain ribbons, to create a truly unique look.

SEE ALSO

page 40: *Ribbons*
page 134: *Sewing on trims*

Q. CAN YOU MAKE LACE?

A. Yes, lace making is an ancient craft. You can crochet simple lace edgings or create more elaborate lace trims using traditional tatting.

PIPING, WELTING AND CORDED EDGES

Piping, welting and corded edgings are trims that have a rounded edge and a flat lip that is stitched into a seam. Piping is smaller and used on garments while welting is larger and is a term usually reserved for home decorating.

Types of piping and welting

Piping is usually 3mm (⅛in) with a lip that is 1.3 to 1.6cm (½in to ⅝in) wide. Welting is bigger at 6mm to 2.5cm (¼in to 1in) wide with a lip that is 1.3 to 1.6cm (½in to ⅝in) wide. It is either made with a bias strip of fabric folded over a cord or is a braided edging.

Most commonly seen on

Piping is commonly used on clothing to emphasise seams and style lines. You see it on necklines, garment edges and armholes. Many Western-style shirts use piping. It is also used on pillows and slipcovers, and upholstery.

Where to get it

You can buy pre-packaged piping in a variety of colours at any fabric store. You may also be able to find it sold by the metre, but you will find the biggest selection at fabric stores that sell fashion fabrics. You can also find a good selection online.

Every sewer should know

Piping and welting can be stitched on using either a zipper foot or a piping or welting foot.

SEE ALSO

page 19: *Presser feet: zipper feet*
page 128: *Bias tape*
page 132: *Piping and welting*

L to R: handmade 6mm (¼in) cotton welting, ready-made 3mm (⅛in) cotton/polyester piping, ready-made polyester corded edge

Q. CAN YOU MAKE PIPING?

A. Yes, you can make your own piping using either store-bought bias tape or your own handmade bias tape.

Q. WHAT IS FLAT PIPING?

A. Flat piping is piping without the inserted cord. It is applied in the same way as corded piping.

POM POM, FRINGES AND RUFFLES

Pom pom fringe, fringe and ruffled trims are all edges that form a decorative embellishment.

Types of pom pom, fringe and ruffles

This is a broad category but all of them are edgings. They can be made out of nearly any fibre and in any colour. Pom pom (also known as ball fringe) can be 100-percent cotton or synthetic. It is characterised by the balls hanging from a braided edge and sometimes has loops interspersed with the balls. Ruffles can really be anything from a ruffled ribbon to lace to fabric ruffles.

Most commonly seen on

Fringe is frequently seen on Western-style apparel but can also be seen on 1920s vintage styles as well as in home decoration. Pom pom is seen on hems, curtains and pillows. Ruffles are seen everywhere from pillows to dress hems, sleeves and necklines.

Where to get it

Pom pom, fringe and ruffles are sold by the metre at any fabric store but you will find the biggest selection at fabric stores that specialise in fashion fabrics. You can also find a good selection online.

Every sewer should know

All fringes and ruffled edges can be sewn into a seam or topstitched on to an edge. Make sure that you check for shrinkage and colourfastness before using.

SEE ALSO

page 40: Ribbons
page 134: Sewing on trims

L to R: cotton pom-pom fringe, handmade ruffles

Q. CAN YOU MAKE RUFFLED TRIMS?

A. Yes, ruffles are very easy to make using a ruffler attachment, or you can use a long gathering stitch and gather by hand. You can ruffle up ribbons or work with strips of fabric. Experiment with the amount that you ruffle up for different effects.

RIBBONS

Ribbons are narrow bands of fabric with specially finished edges to prevent fraying.

Types of ribbon

Satin ribbons are very shiny and can be made of silk or polyester. Single-faced satin ribbon has a right and wrong side while double faced is shiny on both sides. Satin ribbon is available in solid colours in every colour of the rainbow and also in patterns, and comes in a variety of widths from 3mm (⅛in) wide to 7.6cm (3in) wide or more for sashes. Velvet ribbon can be made from silk or synthetics such as polyester. It is also available in single-faced and double-faced options and comes in lots of solid colours and widths. Grosgrain is characterised by its vertical ribs and is available in a variety of solid colours and widths. Sheer ribbons include organza and organdy ribbons. They come in just as many widths as satin ribbons and are available in solids, ombres and patterns. Jacquard ribbons have woven patterns in them. They tend to come in widths ranging from 1 to 5cm (⅜in to 2in) wide. There are a huge amount of patterns available.

Most commonly seen on

Ribbons are used in many ways. They can be stitched on as embellishments or used functionally as sashes, drawstrings, straps, lacing and ties.

Where to get it

You can buy ribbons by the yard or by the roll at any fabric store.

Every sewer should know

You can stitch down narrow ribbons quickly by using a twin needle. Narrow ribbons can also be positioned and stitched using a sequin and ribbon foot.

SEE ALSO

page 24: *Machine needles*
page 134: *Sewing on trims*

L to R: grosgrain ribbon, satin ribbon, jacquard floral ribbon, grosgrain ribbon, velvet ribbon

Q. CAN YOU MAKE RIBBON?

A. Yes, you can layer different widths and types of ribbons to make your own custom ribbon at a fraction of the cost of novelty layered ribbons.

RICKRACK

Also called ric rak or rick-rack, rickrack is made by braiding thread into a flat, zigzag-shaped tape. It is used as a trim on clothes and curtains. Typically, rickrack is made from polyester in a single colour and has a dull or matte finish. Vintage rickracks are usually cotton or a cotton and polyester blend. Rickrack can also be metallic, glossy or variegated with strips or gradations of colour. Some manufacturers add decorative details with embroidery or paint to make rickrack more colourful.

Assorted rickrack

Most commonly seen on

Rickrack is often used on quilts and curtains, but it is flexible enough to be used for almost any project your imagination suggests. You can attach it along the hem of an item, apply it as a top trim, or insert halfway into a seam to create a scalloped edge.

Where to get it

Most craft and fabric stores sell rickrack, usually in an assortment of colours and patterns to meet crafting needs. In some cases, the material is available by the yard. Other stores sell rickrack in pre-packaged lengths, which can result in an excess of unused rickrack.

Every sewer should know

Other thread, such as silk or cotton, may be used, but the resulting rickrack may work out more costly.

SEE ALSO
page 134: Sewing on trims

Q. CAN YOU MAKE RICKRACK?

A. Yes, the simplest options are to knit or crochet it with fine needles using thread that can hold its shape.

Q. HOW DO YOU APPLY RICKRACK?

A. Rickrack is usually applied by hand using thread that matches the item being decorated. If you're not much for handsewing, it can also be straight stitched through the middle by machine, or if the item you're making won't be washed, simply glue on the rickrack.

Closures and fasteners

BUTTONS

Buttons are fasteners used to connect two layers or edges with the button inserted and secured through a buttonhole.

Types of buttons

There are two types: a sew-through button with two to four holes through which to stitch it, and a shank style with a loop on the back. Buttons come in countless colours and are made of materials including plastic, wood, fabric, glass and metal. While typically round, they can be made in other shapes. Some buttons are utilitarian and others are fancy and decorative.

Assorted shank and sew-through buttons

Most commonly seen on

Buttons are used functionally on shirts, jackets, trousers and skirts but they can also be used as embellishment. Buttons are used in accessories such as bags and in home decoration projects such as pillows.

Where to get it

Buttons are available pre-packaged at any fabric store but some stores also sell them loose so that you can pick out the exact number you need. Vintage buttons are available at antique shops and online.

Every sewer should know

Buttons are measured in lignes (pronounced 'lines' and abbreviated L), with 40 lignes equal to 2.5cm (1in).

Q. CAN YOU MAKE BUTTONS?

A. Yes, covered buttons are fun and easy to make. You can get a covered button kit at any fabric store.

Q. CAN YOU SEW BUTTONS ON BY MACHINE?

A. Yes, sew-through buttons can be sewn on by machine but shank buttons need to be stitched on by hand.

LIGNE TO IMPERIAL AND METRIC CONVERSION TABLE

LIGNE	18	20	22	24	28	30	32	34	36	40
METRIC	10 mm	13 mm	14 mm	16 mm	18 mm	19 mm	21 mm	22 mm	22 mm	25 mm
INCH	3/8	1/2	9/16	5/8	11/16	3/4	5/6	6/7	7/8	1

SEE ALSO

page 19: *Buttonhole and button feet*
page 174: *Buttons*

HARDWARE

Hardware in sewing refers to metal notions such as buckles, sliders, eyelets, grommets, O-rings, D-rings and other types of rings. Hardware can be very simple with a plain finish or embellished with rhinestones and other designs.

Most commonly seen on

You see hardware often on outerwear, curtains, corsets, handbags and accessories such as belts.

Types of hardware

Buckles are used to fasten two ends together and allow for an adjustable closure. They have a frame and a prong that catches in a hole to secure it. Sliders are basically a buckle without a prong – a strip of fabric slides over the centre bar. Narrow strips of fabric or trims can be threaded through rings, which can be functional or purely decorative. Eyelets and grommets are rings of metal used to reinforce a hole in a piece of fabric. Eyelets are small while grommets are large.

Where to get it

You can purchase hardware at most fabric stores. You can buy pre-packaged eyelets, rings and buckles or you may also be able to find them sold loose. You can also buy hardware at the hardware store!

Every sewer should know

Usually hardware is available only in silver and gold tones but sometimes you can find other colours such as antique brass and antique nickel.

SEE ALSO

page 19: Buttonhole and button feet
page 175: Grommets and eyelets
page 179: Buckles
page 180: D-rings and O-rings

Clockwise from top: O-ring, buckle, slider, eyelets and grommets, buckle, D-ring

Q. HOW DO YOU ATTACH EYELETS?

A. Eyelets and grommets are sold in kits with a setting tool and you can hammer them in according to the instructions. Many can also be inserted using special pliers. You can also purchase refills if you need more.

Q. CAN YOU STITCH RINGS DIRECTLY ON TO FABRIC?

A. Yes, rings can be stitched down using a button foot and a zigzag stitch.

HOOKS AND EYES

Hooks and eyes are fasteners to connect either edges that meet or edges that overlap. They are sold in sets and each set has a small metal hook that connects to a matching ring or bar called the eye. Hooks and eyes are available in black, white, silver and gold.

Most commonly seen on

Hooks and eyes are most often used at the top of zips on skirts and dresses, on corsets and on lingerie.

Types of hooks and eyes

Hook and eye sets come with a hook and two types of eyes. The round eye is used for edges that meet while the bar eye is used for edges that overlap. Most hooks and eyes are handstitched on, but you can also get sets that clamp on. Hooks and eyes come in many different sizes ranging from a tiny size 0 to a large size 3. There are also extra-large hooks and eyes for coats.

Where to get it

Any fabric store sells hooks and eyes. You can get a package of assorted sizes or all one size.

Every sewer should know

Bra backs are ready-made notions that have hooks and eyes attached to materials. They can be used to extend or repair bras.

> **SEE ALSO**
>
> *page 22: Handsewing needles*
> *page 181: Hooks and eyes*

Assorted hooks and eyes

Q. I DON'T LIKE HANDSEWING. CAN I MACHINE STITCH HOOKS AND EYES?

A. Yes, you can use hook-and-eye tape. This is either a tape or narrow fabric with the hooks on one piece and the eyes on the other. You can machine stitch the tape in place. If you can't find hook-and-eye tape in the right colour, then you can dye it.

SNAPS

Snaps are fasteners that are used to connect overlapping edges and can be used instead of buttons.

Types of snaps

There are sew-on snaps and no-sew snaps. Sew-on snaps are a two-part snap with one side called the ball and the other called the socket. The ball portion is used on the overlapping edge and the socket on the underlapping edge; they are handstitched on through the little holes around the perimeter. Snaps are usually metal and are available in silver, gold and black. They come in assorted sizes ranging from very small size 1 up to extra-large size 10. They are sold on cards, with either all one size or an assortment of sizes per card. No-sew snaps include pearl snaps that have prongs to grip the fabric and are hammered in place, and heavy-duty snaps that can be hammered in place with a setter or applied with special pliers. No-sew snaps are sized just like buttons.

Most commonly seen on

Snaps are used on shirts and tops, jackets, waistbands and accessories such as wallets.

Where to get it

Any fabric store should sell a variety of snaps for any sewing need.

Every sewer should know

You can get snap-fastener kits that include a variety of no-sew snaps and some pliers.

SEE ALSO

page 22: *Handsewing needles*
page 44: *Hooks and eyes*
page 176: *Snaps*

L to R: no-sew snaps, sew-on snaps

Q. MY PATTERN CALLS FOR BUTTONS AND BUTTONHOLES. CAN I USE SNAPS INSTEAD?

A. Absolutely! This is a great way to customise a design and really make it your own.

Q. I NEED TO APPLY A LOT OF SNAPS ON A GARMENT. DO I REALLY NEED TO HANDSEW THEM ON? CAN'T I GLUE THEM?

A. No, don't glue them as the glue might clog the sockets and prevent them from fastening correctly. Instead, try using snap tape. It is stitched on just like hook-and-eye tape.

HOOK-AND-LOOP FASTENERS

Hook-and-loop fasteners (commonly known by the brand name Velcro) are used to fasten overlapping edges and are closed by simply laying the pieces on top of each other. Hook-and-loop fasteners have two parts: one side has little hooks and the other side has plush loops. To open, the parts are pulled apart.

Most commonly seen on

Hook-and-loop fasteners are often used on children's wear because they're easy for kids to handle. They are also used on closures that need to be adjustable.

Types of hook-and-loop fasteners

Hook-and-loop fasteners come in strips, squares and dots and are also sold by the metre. They are usually available only in black, white and beige but sometimes you can find them in other colours. The fasteners come in different sizes and widths, in sew-on, self-adhesive and fusible varieties.

Where to get it

You can buy the dots, squares and strips at any fabric or craft store. Good fabric stores will also have it available by the yard and may also have fashion colours.

Every sewer should know

Never sew through stick-on fasteners because the adhesive will gum up your needle very quickly. Also, be careful to keep unused fasteners wrapped because otherwise the hook side will catch on fabrics and threads and make a big mess.

SEE ALSO

page 18: *Basic feet*
page 28: *All-purpose sewing thread*
page 178: *Hook-and-loop tape*

Hook-and-loop dots, strips and squares

Q. HOW DO I SEW ON HOOK-AND-LOOP TAPE?

A. There is a little lip along the edge that you can stitch along using an all-purpose foot and thread.

ZIPS

Zips have teeth attached to a tape that are closed with a slider attached to a zip pull. They are used to join edges that meet.

Most commonly seen on

Zips are used on many garments such as trousers, skirts and dresses. They can be used on pockets or as a closure for a whole garment. They are used extensively on handbags, luggage, pillows and slipcovers.

Types of zips

Standard zips have coil teeth or moulded teeth. The teeth can be made of nylon, polyester, plastic or metal and the tape comes in a huge variety of colours and lengths. Invisible zips have the teeth concealed on the back side and a tiny teardrop pull. Separating zips open at the bottom for garments that need to open completely while standard and invisible zips are closed at the bottom and are for seams, such as on a skirt. Dual or two-way zips have two sliders and can open from the top or bottom; these are great for handbags, slipcovers and sleeping bags. Reversible zips have a pull that can flip to either side and are made for reversible garments. You can get novelty zips with rainbow or jewelled teeth and fancy tapes.

Where to get it

Any craft and fabric store will sell basic zips but you may need to go to a good fabric store for novelty and speciality zips.

Every sewer should know

You can always shorten a zip but you cannot lengthen one. If you cannot find the right length zip in the colour you want, get a longer one and shorten it.

SEE ALSO

page 19: Zipper feet
page 182: Zips

L to R: nylon coil zipper, metal zip, molded plastic teeth zip, invisible zip, nylon coil zip

Q. DO I NEED AN INVISIBLE ZIPPER FOOT TO USE AN INVISIBLE ZIP?

A. No, but it does make it easier and more precise. You can use a standard zipper foot to install an invisible zip if necessary.

Q. WHAT IF I NEED A SUPER-LONG ZIP?

A. You can buy zips by the metre at good fabric stores. It will come with a slider and pull.

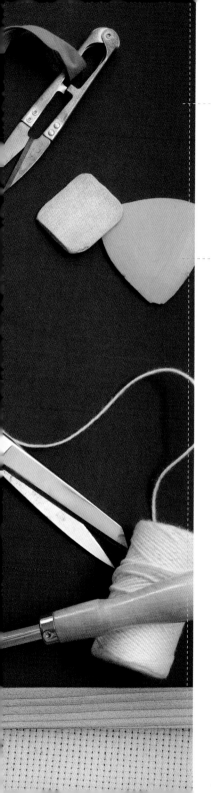

CHAPTER 3
MARKING,
MEASURING AND
CUTTING TOOLS

In addition to your basic sewing machine, needles and thread, there are other tools that you will use every time you sew. You need to cut fabric, threads and trims. You need to measure flat items, such as fabrics, and also people. And finally, accurate marks make sewing easier and faster. In this chapter, we will go over all the different types of tools that will make these jobs a breeze.

Tailor's chalk

Tailor's chalk is a special chalk made of talc that makes temporary marks on fabric. When the marks are no longer needed, they can be brushed or washed away. Tailor's chalk comes in a variety of colours including white, yellow, blue and pink. Use a colour that contrasts with your fabric.

Most commonly used for
Tailor's chalk can be used to mark design details such as buttonholes and button placement, darts and pleats, seam lines, folds and alteration lines.

Types of tailor's chalk
Tailor's chalk comes in pencils, wedges and wheels. Each type has its pros and cons. The pencils can be hard and drag on your fabric but they can be sharpened so you always have a fine line. The wedges mark well but the point wears down and can make too wide a mark when you need precision. The chalk wheels use loose chalk to make a very fine line. The wheel does not pull on your fabric but the loose chalk brushes away very easily and you might accidentally brush away your marks.

Where to get it
Any fabric store will carry a variety of tailor's chalk.

Every sewer should know
Be careful when ironing over chalk marks. Sometimes the heat of the iron can set the dyes in the chalk, and the marks won't come out in the wash. When in doubt, always do a test on a scrap of fabric.

SEE ALSO ⟩·
page 98: Marking fabric
Chapter 9: Fitting solutions

L to R: Chalk wedge, chalk pencil, chalk wedges, chalk wheel

Q. ARE DIFFERENT TYPES OF CHALK BETTER FOR CERTAIN FABRICS?

A. Pencils work well for stable and flat fabrics such as quilting cotton. Wheels and wedges, which don't pull, work better with stretchy or plush fabrics.

Markers and pens

Fabric markers and pens use ink to make temporary or permanent marks.

Most commonly used for
Fabric markers and pens can be used to mark all the same design details as chalk.

Types of fabric markers and pens
Temporary markers use ink that is either air-soluble, water-soluble, or both. Air-soluble (also known as air-erasable or vanishing) ink marks will disappear over time, usually within two to fourteen days. Water-soluble ink can be washed away with water. Markers and pens come in different colours, with the air-soluble types traditionally available in purple and the water-soluble pens in blue. They can also be found in other colours such as white and pink. Permanent markers make marks that don't come out so they should not be used to mark design details, but can be used to trace patterns on to fabrics.

Where to get it
Any good fabric store will carry different types of fabric markers and pens. Experiment with the different types until you find the ones that work best for you and the fabric type you are working with.

Every sewer should know
Be careful when ironing over ink marks. Sometimes the heat of the iron can permanently set the dyes in the ink and the marks won't come out in the wash. When in doubt, always do a test on a scrap of fabric. Also, fabric markers tend to dry out very fast, so make sure to cap them tightly when you're not using them.

> **SEE ALSO** ›·
> **page 98:** Marking fabric
> **Chapter 9:** Fitting solutions

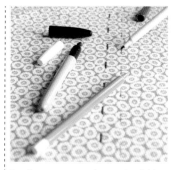

L to R: permanent marker, water-soluble marker, air-soluble marker

Q. I'M USING AN AIR-SOLUBLE MARKER AND I'M AFRAID MY MARKS WILL DISAPPEAR BY THE TIME I NEED THEM.

A. Seal your project in a closeable plastic bag, which will prevent air from reaching the marks, or put adhesive tape over them.

Tracing wheels

Tracing wheels have either a smooth, serrated or pointy metal wheel attached to a wood or plastic handle.

Most commonly used for

They are used with transfer or carbon paper to transfer design details and markings to fabric, for copying a pattern on to other paper and for pattern making.

Types of tracing wheels

Smooth and serrated tracing wheels are used together with transfer paper to mark directly on fabric, and you can use them to mark design details in the same way as you would use chalk and pens. The smooth wheels leave a solid line and work well with delicate tissue patterns. The serrated wheels leave a dotted line and can work with both tissue and heavier paper patterns. The needlepoint tracing wheels have extremely sharp teeth and are used in pattern making to mark through fabric on to pattern paper with perforations. They are also extremely useful for making patterns from existing garments when you don't want to take the garment apart. Instead, you run the wheel along the seam lines to leave perforations in the pattern paper. The points won't damage fabric or the garment.

Where to get it

The smooth and serrated tracing wheels are easily found at most fabric stores, but the needlepoint tracing wheels are only available in good fabric stores and those that carry pattern-making supplies. You can also purchase them online.

Every sewer should know

The needlepoint tracing wheels are very sharp, so be careful with them! It's best to keep them stored in the original box or sheath for safety's sake.

SEE ALSO
page 98: Marking fabric

L to R: needlepoint tracing wheels, serrated tracing wheels

TIP

Low-priced wheels tend to be a little wobbly and make it difficult to trace lines accurately. It is best to buy a good quality, sturdy wheel.

Transfer paper

Transfer paper (also known as dressmaker's tracing paper) is a sheet of paper coated with pigment.

Most commonly used for

It is used in conjunction with a tracing wheel to transfer design details from a pattern directly to fabric. You slip the transfer paper between the pattern and fabric and then, using a smooth or serrated tracing wheel, run the wheel along the lines you want to transfer and the pigment transfers from the paper to the fabric.

Types of transfer paper

Transfer paper comes in assorted sizes in sheets or in rolls. The pigment is either chalky or waxy and it comes in various colours including white, yellow, blue, red and orange. Most transfer paper is single-sided but you can also find double-sided transfer paper.

Where to get it

Transfer paper is sold in the notions department at any fabric store or you can also find it in art supply stores.

Every sewer should know

Just like with other marking tools, always test transfer paper on a scrap of your fabric to make sure the marks are removable and don't iron over them at the risk of heat setting them. Also, the chalk paper can be a little messy so be careful not to smear it across your fabric.

SEE ALSO ⟩·
page 98: Marking fabric

Assorted colours of transfer paper with a serrated tracing wheel

Q. CAN I MARK BOTH LAYERS OF FABRIC AT THE SAME TIME?

A. Yes, you can either use double-sided transfer paper or fold the transfer paper in half so that the pigmented sides are against both layers of fabric.

Basic measuring tools

Rulers, tape measures and seam gauges are basic measuring tools that everyone should have in their sewing box. They are used to measure fabric, people, seams and more. They have measurements marked in metric, imperial or both.

Most commonly used for
Tape measures are used to take measurements of three-dimensional objects, such as the human body. Flat measuring devices, including rulers and seam gauges, are used to measure flat items such as fabric and patterns.

Types of basic rulers
Basic tape measures are either made of cloth, vinyl, or fibreglass. They come in various lengths; 152cm (60in) long is the most common but longer lengths, such as 305cm (120in), are also available. They have inches marked on one side and centimetres on the other. You can also get retractable tape measures, but standard tape measures are the easiest to work with. A clear 5 x 46cm (2in x 18in) ruler is invaluable for adding on seam allowances, measuring hems and seams and more. It is flexible and can be gently bent around curved edges. Rulers are clearly marked with either metric or imperial measurements but are rarely marked with both. A 15cm (6in) seam gauge has a little sliding marker to maintain accurate measurements and is frequently used to mark hems and buttonhole placement.

Where to get it
Basic tape measures and rulers are available in the notions department of any fabric store.

Every sewer should know
A fibreglass tape measure is the best type because it won't stretch over time and maintains accuracy.

SEE ALSO
Chapter 9: Fitting solutions

Top to Bottom: tape measure, seam gauge, 5 by 46cm ruler

Q. DO I NEED A YARDSTICK?
A. No, I find that the traditional wooden yardstick is not all that useful. Clear acrylic grid rulers are much better because you can see through them when measuring and they help you line up items faster and more accurately.

Speciality measuring tools

Speciality rulers may not get used every day but are a useful addition to your tool box. They include curved rulers, such as French curves and design rulers, flexible rulers and clear acrylic grid rulers.

Types of speciality rulers
French curves and design rulers (also known as fashion rulers) have various curved edges to draw in necklines, armholes, hip curves and sleeves; some have measurements on them. They are used extensively during patternmaking and also when altering and fitting existing patterns. Flexible rulers have a core that can be easily bent and maintain the curve for accurate drawing, and they have measurements on them.

Acrylic grid rulers are clear, rigid rulers with measurements and are designed to be used with rotary cutters. The acrylic prevents the rotary blade from damaging and gouging the ruler. Acrylic grid rulers come in different sizes and shapes, and many of them are also printed with different angles, for example, a 45-degree angle. They are very popular with quilters. My favourite is a 15 x 61cm (6in x 24in) rectangle.

Where to get it
Specialty rulers are sold at fabric stores but you can also get them at art-supply and craft stores.

Every sewer should know
It is best to buy a large acrylic grid ruler rather than getting several at smaller sizes. It will be more versatile.

SEE ALSO ➔
page 57: *Rotary cutters and mats*
page 96: *Cutting fabric*
Chapter 9: *Fitting solutions*

L to R: Design ruler, flexible ruler, acrylic grid ruler, French curve

Q. IF I WANT TO PICK ONE CURVED RULER, WHICH ONE IS THE MOST VERSATILE?

A. The design ruler is definitely the most versatile. It has the greatest variety of curved edges plus a straight edge and 90-degree angle with measurements everywhere. I use mine constantly. If you can't find a design ruler, then French curves are a good substitute.

Cutting tools

SCISSORS

For sewing you need three types of scissors: dressmaker's shears, small scissors and pinking shears.

Types of scissors

Dressmaker's shears are used to cut fabric. The most common size is 20cm (8in), measured from tip to handle. They have angled handles to allow the bottom blade and your fabric to lay flat against the table when cutting and they should be able to cut all the way to the tip. You also need a small pair of scissors, such as thread snips or embroidery scissors, to trim threads, cut open buttonholes and cut snips and notches. Pinking shears have a notched edge on the blades and are used to finish seam allowances to help prevent fraying.

Where to get it

All fabric stores carry scissors but you can also purchase them from cutlery stores.

Every sewer should know

Fabric scissors are among the most important and frequently used tools you will own, so invest in a quality pair. They cost anywhere from £15 to £30 but they will last a lifetime. Never use your fabric scissors to cut anything but fabric and thread. It is worth getting scissors sharpened once a year. Hardware stores, cutlery stores and some fabric stores offer scissor sharpening services.

SEE ALSO

page 96: Cutting fabric
page 98: Marking fabric
page 108: Seam allowance

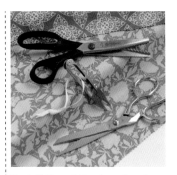

Top to Bottom: pinking shears, thread snips, dressmaker's shears

TIP

If you are left handed, look for left-handed scissors. If you have arthritis in your hands, look for spring-handled or electric scissors; they are easier on the tendons in the hands.

ROTARY CUTTERS AND MATS

Rotary cutters have a razor-sharp retractable round blade attached to a handle. The round blade easily cuts through multiple layers of fabric. They must be used together with a cutting mat to prevent damage to tables and to prolong the life of the blade. You also need a special ruler designed to work with rotary cutters to use as a straight-edge guide.

Most commonly used for
Rotary cutters are used to cut out patterns and fabrics.

Types of rotary cutters and mats
Rotary cutters come with different-size blades ranging from 18mm, 45mm, to 60mm in diameter. The 45mm cutter is the most commonly used, with the smaller size better for detail work and the bigger size for long, straight cuts. The blades need to be replaced frequently. If you are going to use a rotary cutter for most of your cutting, look into purchasing a bulk pack of replacement blades to save money. The handles can be straight or shaped for better ergonomics – find a handle that fits comfortably in your hand.

The cutting mats come in a range of sizes. I find that the 61 x 91cm (24in x 36in) is an ideal size for most sewing projects. These mats are marked with grid lines and useful angles such as 30, 45, and 60 degrees and have a non-skid base.

Where to get it
Rotary cutters and mats are sold at fabric and craft stores.

Every sewer should know
Take care using rotary cutters. You should always cut away from yourself and stand up for a better grip and visibility. Always use the safety latch when you put down the cutter.

Rotary cutter and mat

TIP
Never throw old blades into the garbage but dispose of them in the original case or in a plastic container.

SEE ALSO
page 55: Speciality measuring tools
page 96: Cutting fabric
page 98: Marking fabric

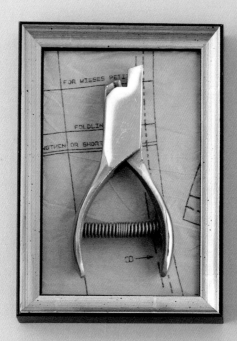

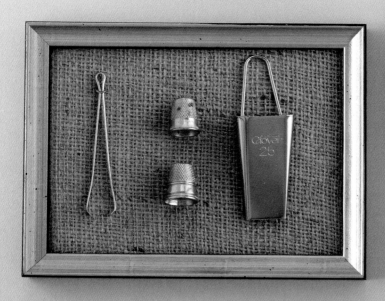

CHAPTER 4
MISCELLANEOUS TOOLS

If you are the sort of person who loves gadgets, then you will love this chapter. Here, you'll discover all the helpful little tools that make even the most mundane sewing task a joy.

Pins

Pins are made of metal and have plastic, glass or metal heads.

Most commonly used for

Pins are used to hold fabric layers together for sewing and fitting. They are also used to position and hold pockets, appliqués, trims and zips in place for sewing.

Types of pins

General-purpose sewing pins have a sharp point and range from 2.5 to 3.8cm (1in to 1½in) long. Silk pins have very thin shafts of only 0.5mm (0.02in) so they won't create large holes in fabrics. Ballpoint pins have rounded points to slide between fibres to avoid damaging knit fabrics. Appliqué pins are very short – 1.3 to 1.9cm (½in to ¾in) long. Quilting pins are 3.8 to 5cm (1½in to 2in) long, and are designed for lofty fabrics.

Where to get it

You can buy pins at fabric, quilting and craft stores.

Every sewer should know

Good-quality pins are worth the money because they will not snag and damage fabrics. Many professional seamstresses use pins with glass heads; you can safely iron over them and the heads will not melt.

SEE ALSO
page 98: Marking fabric
Chapter 7: Sewing solutions

Top: *Top to Bottom: plastic-head pins, glass-head silk pins, appliqué pins, quilting pins*
Bottom: *Assorted pin cushions*

TIP

Pincushions provide a place to safely store pins and allow easy access while sewing and fitting. The traditional red tomato pincushion is tightly stuffed with sawdust and wool roving to prevent rusting of the pins, with an emery-filled strawberry to sharpen them. Wrist pin cushions are convenient during fittings and handsewing. You can also buy magnetic pincushions.

Seam rippers

A seam ripper is a tool with a sharp, forked end attached to a handle. The fork has one sharp point to allow easy insertion in tight stitches and one with a ballpoint to protect fabric.

Most commonly used for
Seam rippers are used to remove unwanted stitches. The sharp point allows you to rip out threads without damaging the fabric. You can also use a seam ripper to cut open buttonholes after they have been stitched.

Types of seam rippers
Seam rippers come in different sizes and with different handle shapes, such as ergonomic handles. You can also find surgical seam rippers that look like a utility knife with a curved blade. These can be used to rip out serger stitches.

Where to get it
Your sewing machine likely came with a seam ripper but this type is often low quality with a dull blade. You can buy seam rippers at fabric, quilting and craft stores.

Every sewer should know
Never use scissors to rip out stitches because it's very easy to accidently cut the fabric.

A standard seam ripper

TIP
Replace your seam ripper periodically as the blade gets dull and cannot be sharpened.

Point turners

A point turner is a tool with a slightly pointed end designed to gently push out corners on pillows, pockets, collars and more. It also has a rounded end to push out curved edges and to flatten seam allowances.

Types of point turners
Point turners are made of either plastic or wood, frequently bamboo.

Where to get it
You can buy point turners at any fabric store.

Every sewer should know
Never use your scissors to poke out corners or you risk poking a hole right through the fabric.

: SEE ALSO :·
Chapter 7: *Sewing solutions*
page 126: *Pockets*
page 170: *Buttonholes*
page 174: *Buttons*

L to R: plastic point turner, bamboo point turner

TIPS
A knitting needle or chopstick can make a great point turner because it has a blunt point and won't cut through fabric.

A bamboo point turner can be used as a pressing tool because you can iron over it.

Loop turners

A loop turner has a long wand attached to a handle with a latch-hook-shaped end.

Most commonly used for
Loop turners are used for turning tubes of fabric for purse handles, spaghetti straps and drawstrings. You stitch a tube of fabric, insert the wand through the tube, hook the latch on the end, close the hook and pull the fabric down through the tube to turn it right side out.

Types of loop turners
The most common type is the latch-hook wand. Sets of hollow cylinders are also available in various sizes, with a separate, specially designed wire with a spiral tip. You slip the cylinder through your fabric tube and use the wire to pull the fabric down though the cylinder. Another type is a flat plastic turner with a clip on the end. You clip the fabric on the end and then push the fabric down through the tube to turn it right side out.

Where to get it
You can buy loop turners in the notions department at fabric stores.

Every sewer should know
Once you master the loop turner, it is the fastest method for turning tubes.

L to R: latch-hook style loop turner, plastic clip and turner

Bodkins

There are two types of bodkins: one looks like tweezers with teeth on the ends and a ring to hold it clamped shut. The other looks like an extra-large needle with a large eye and a ballpoint.

Most commonly used for

Bodkins are designed to quickly and easily pull elastics, cords, ribbons and drawstrings through casings. With a needle bodkin, you thread the cord through the eye and then pull through the casing. The tweezer type is for items that are too large for needle bodkins. You clamp the item in the teeth, slide the ring down to hold it firmly and then thread through the casing.

Where to get it

Bodkins are found in the notions department at fabric stores.

Every sewer should know

Thread items through casings slowly and carefully so they stay in the bodkin.

SEE ALSO
page 153: *Waistline*

L to R: tweezer-style bodkin, needle-style bodkin

TIP

You can also use a large safety pin for the job, but be careful because it can easily come open and get caught in the casing.

Seam sealant

Seam sealant is a fast-drying liquid that is applied to fabric edges to prevent fraying. It dries clear and flexible and can be washed and dry-cleaned.

Most commonly used for
Seam sealant is used on raw edges, seams, corners and cord ends, as well as buttonholes and the ends of ribbons and trims.

Where to get it
You can buy seam sealant in the notion section at fabric stores.

Every sewer should know
Apply a tiny drop using the applicator or a toothpick. It can be removed using rubbing alcohol. Seam sealant will not discolour most fabrics but it is a good idea to test on a scrap first. Some seam sealants are flammable, so follow the directions carefully.

SEE ALSO
page 138: *Fabric appliqué*
page 162: *Hems*
page 170: *Buttonholes*
page 174: *Buttons*

A couple of brands of seam sealant

Q. CAN YOU USE CLEAR NAIL POLISH AS A SEAM SEALANT?

A. Yes, but it can dry very stiff and shiny.

TIP
You may find it helpful to use a thimble. A thimble is a protective cover worn over the finger when handsewing to help push a needle through layers of fabric. It can be made of metal, plastic, ceramic, leather or rubber. Open-ended thimbles are good for people with long nails. Thimbles come in various sizes; a thimble should fit comfortably and stay in place. If your metal thimble does not fit comfortably, squeeze it a little to make it slightly oval.

Bias tape makers: manual

A bias tape maker is a hand-held tool that makes single-fold bias tape in the fabric of your choice. Just slip the bias strip in the end of the maker and pull the handle. The bias strip is folded over as it feeds through the device, and the folds are then pressed into place with your iron. See page 76 for an explanation of bias grain.

Most commonly used for

Bias tape can be used to finish curved edges on necklines, armholes and hems, or to bind edges on quilts, bibs and garments.

Types of manual bias tape makers

Manual bias tape makers come in various widths including 6mm (¼in), 1.3cm (½in), 1.9cm (¾in), 2.5cm (1in) and 5cm (2in).

Where to get it

You can buy manual bias tape makers at fabric, quilting and craft stores.

Every sewer should know

The most useful sizes are 1.3cm (½in) to make standard single-fold bias tape, 2.5cm (1in) to make wide single-fold bias tape and double-fold bias tape and 5cm (2in) to make double-fold quilt binding.

SEE ALSO

page 34: Bias tape
page 76: Grainlines and bias
page 128: Bias tape
page 162: Hems

L to R: 2.5cm (1in) bias tape maker; 1.3cm (½in) bias tape maker

Q. HOW DO YOU MAKE DOUBLE-FOLD BIAS TAPE WITH A BIAS TAPE MAKER?

A. If you want double-fold bias tape, make single-fold bias tape that is twice the desired width. Fold it in half with one side slightly wider, and iron.

Bias tape-making machines

Bias tape-making machines fold bias strips of fabric and press them into bias tape with the push of a button. They have a built-in iron and a winding wheel to hold the bias strips. The machine feeds the bias strips from the wheel through the bias tip and across the ironing plate to make the bias tape automatically.

Most commonly used for
These machines are used for making large quantities of bias tape much faster than using a manual bias tape maker. It is advertised that they can make 30cm (12in) of bias tape in as little as sixty seconds! Bias tape-making machines come equipped with a tip to make 2.5cm (1in) single-fold bias tape but you can purchase additional tip sizes separately. The other sizes available include 1cm (³⁄₈in), 1.3cm (¹⁄₂in), 1.9cm (³⁄₄in) and 3.2cm (1¹⁄₄in).

Where to get it
Bias tape-making machines can be found at larger chain fabric stores and online.

Every sewer should know
If you just need custom bias tape for a single project, the manual bias tape maker might be a better choice. But if you use bias tape all the time, you might want to invest in one of these machines.

SEE ALSO
page 34: Bias tape
page 76: Grainlines and bias
page 128: Bias tape
page 162: Hems

Bias tape-making machine with a 2.5cm (1in) tip

Q. CAN YOU MAKE DOUBLE-FOLD BIAS TAPE WITH A BIAS TAPE-MAKING MACHINE?

A. If you want double-fold bias tape, make single-fold bias tape that is twice the desired width, then fold it in half with one side slightly wider and run it under the iron on the machine again.

Pattern paper

Pattern paper is a strong paper that is used to duplicate and alter sewing patterns and to create original patterns.

Types of pattern paper
The most common type, also called marker paper, is white with dots or letters and numbers arranged in a 2.5cm (1in) grid. It is translucent so that you can see pattern lines through it to copy them. It comes on a roll in widths ranging from 110cm to 180cm (45in to 72in) wide and is sold by the metre or by the roll.

Another common pattern paper is oaktag or manila paper. This is a heavier, opaque paper that comes on rolls in the same widths as marker paper. It is designed for production patterns or patterns that are used repeatedly.

Most other types of pattern paper are made from plain white paper, ranging from lightweight tracing paper to heavier-weight bond paper.

Where to get it
Pattern paper can sometimes be found in fabric stores that carry apparel fabrics or pattern-making supplies. You can find it in art supply stores and online.

Every sewer should know
If your pattern paper is wrinkled, you can iron it to smooth it out. Use a medium-hot iron and make sure the steam is turned off.

SEE ALSO
page 98: Marking fabric
Chapter 9: Fitting solutions

L to R: marker paper; oaktag paper

TIP
If you can't find pattern paper, then any sort of paper can be substituted, such as postal paper, medical paper, brown craft paper and wrapping paper.

Pattern notchers and awls

A pattern notcher is a hand-held tool that punches 6 x 1.6mm (¼in x ¹⁄₁₆in) wide slits in the edge of sewing patterns. An awl looks a bit like an ice pick with a long, sharp point attached to a handle.

Most commonly used for

Notchers are used to cut a slit in your pattern where your triangular notches are located. The notches can then be marked with a fabric marker and snipped open to mark seam allowances and positions of darts and pleats. This is much faster and more accurate than cutting around the triangles. Because the notches are so small, they will be hidden in the seam allowance.

Awls are used to pierce holes through patterns at marking where you cannot use a pattern notcher. This hole allows you to mark the position with a marker or chalk directly on your fabric. Common places to mark with an awl are dart points, pocket placements, buttons and buttonholes.

Where to get it

Pattern notchers can be difficult to find in chain fabric stores but you may find them in stores that cater to garment sewers and those that carry pattern-making supplies. They can also be found online.

Awls are sold in the notion department at good fabric stores and those that carry pattern-making supplies. They can also be found online.

Every sewer should know

Never use a pattern notcher on fabric or you will permanently dull the blades.

SEE ALSO

page 98: Marking fabric
Chapter 7: Sewing solutions

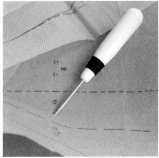

Top: *Professional pattern notcher*
Bottom: *Plastic-handled awl*

TIP

If a professional pattern notcher is out of your budget, check the scrapbooking punches at your local craft store. You can sometimes find punches that make a similar snip shape to a pattern notcher.

TIP

You can use the awl to poke a small hole through fabric as a mark at a dart point. Offset the hole 6mm (¼in) so that it will not show.

Dress forms

A dress form, or dressmakers' dummy, is a three-dimensional replica of the human body used extensively during the design process for fitting patterns and garments.

Types of dress forms

A standard dress form has just the torso and hips but there are also full-body dress forms that include legs, called bifurcated forms. Dress forms do not have arms but you can purchase or make an attachable arm for fitting sleeves.

Forms are sold in different sizes and figure types and are available in junior sizes, missy/ladies' sizes, women's/plus sizes, men's sizes and children's sizes. You can get adjustable forms that have dials to expand panels on the form to accommodate different sizes and shapes. There are also adjustable forms that come with pads so you can pad up a form to replicate different shapes and sizes.

Traditional dress forms used in the garment industry and in fashion design schools are made of papier mâché, padded with cotton wadding and covered with linen. They have an adjustable height and a pinnable surface so you can pin right into the form. Some forms have collapsible shoulders that make it easy to get garments on and off the form. There are also forms that have a more defined bust and buttocks; these are called lingerie or evening-wear forms.

You can also get forms that are a plastic base with a fabric cover – these are usually the adjustable forms with dials. They are not as easy to pin into; instead you secure pins into the fabric cover.

L to R: adjustable dress form, professional dress form, vintage dress form

Most commonly used for

Having a dress form that closely replicates your figure helps you to make pattern alterations to ensure a good fit. Dress forms can also be used to evaluate design details and placement before sewing. You can pin on pockets to establish the most flattering placement, rotate and adjust darts and really experiment before sewing things together.

Dress forms are also used when designing garments from scratch. You can drape fabric on to the form and create your design three dimensionally.

Where to get it

You can buy adjustable dress forms at most chain fabric stores. Professional dress forms are sold in fabric stores and suppliers in the garment districts of major cities or you can order one online. You might get lucky and find one at a carboot sale or a vintage shop!

Every sewer should know

Most dress forms are designed with a B-cup bust and a standard shape. But most of us are not standard. If you are larger than a B cup, you will need to pad up your form. The easiest way to do this is to put one of your bras on the form (not your favourite!) and stuff the cups on the bra. You can also pad out hips and buttocks with quilt batting and add shoulder pads to change the shoulder line.

SEE ALSO
Chapter 8: Embellishment and trimming solutions
Chapter 9: Fitting solutions

Q. CAN YOU MAKE A DRESS FORM?

A. Yes, you can make a dress form out of duct tape, a T-shirt and pillow stuffing. There are lots of tutorials available on the Internet, and many sewing schools offer classes on making duct-tape dress forms.

SECTION TWO
Solutions and Tips

denim

ticking

CANVAS

CHAPTER 5
FABRIC SOLUTIONS

We all love fabric. That's why we took up sewing in the first place! There are so many beautiful and amazing fabrics to choose from, but how to know which is right for your project? Find out about the different types of fabric available, how to identify them and all about supporting materials such as linings and interfacings.

Anatomy of fabric

Fabric is made by weaving, knitting or pressing threads, yarns or fibres together. It comes in an endless variety of colours, patterns, prints, textures and weights for different looks and purposes. Most fabrics used for sewing are woven, made from threads woven over and under each other. Knitted fabrics are made from an interlocking series of loops. Then there are non-woven materials, including leather and suede, and fabrics such as felt that are made by pressing and matting fibres together with heat and steam.

GRAINLINES AND BIAS

Woven fabric is made from threads running in two perpendicular directions. The threads that go from the top to the bottom of the fabric are called the warp threads and form the length grain, while the threads that go from left to right are called the weft threads and form the cross grain. (To remember the difference, I always think to myself 'wight and weft' like Elmer Fudd.) The finished edges along both sides are called the selvage, and the selvages are often printed with the name of the manufacturer. The warp and weft threads should be at 90-degree angles to each other – this is called the fabric being 'on grain'. The warp or length-grain threads are strung on to a loom first and are therefore the tightest and do not give. The weft or cross-grain threads are then woven over and under the warp threads and therefore have a bit of give or 'mechanical stretch'. The bias refers to any diagonal but the true bias is the 45-degree angle between the length and cross grains; the bias has lots of stretch and give.

Knitted fabrics also have length and cross grain even though they do not have warp and weft threads. They still have selvages on either edge and they will have more stretch on the cross grain than the length grain. Non-wovens, such as felt, do not have a grain but may still have a selvage.

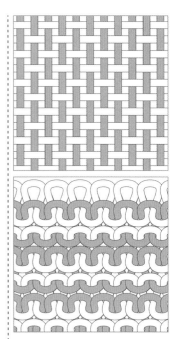

Top: *Woven fabric*
Bottom: *Knitted fabric*

Sometimes fabric is off grain, and the warp and weft are not at right angles to each other. The fabric can look skewed or bowed, which is caused by the fabric being wound unevenly on to a bolt or roll. You can easily straighten the grain by pulling on the bias to realign the warp and weft threads and you should always make sure fabric is on grain before cutting out your pieces. Garments that are cut off grain tend to drape at an odd angle and twist on the body.

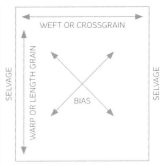

FIBRE CONTENT

Fabric can be made from natural or synthetic fibres, or a blend of both. Natural fibres include plant-based fibres such as cotton and linen, and animal-based fibres such as silk and wool. There are also hair fibres, including cashmere, angora, and alpaca. Eco-friendly fibres, for example, bamboo and organic cotton, are becoming very popular and affordable. Synthetic fibres are made from chemicals or petroleum and include polyester, rayon, nylon, acetate, acrylic and spandex. Many synthetic fibres were created as a cheaper substitute for natural fibres. Nylon was invented as a substitute for silk, while acrylic was developed as a substitute for wool. Other synthetic fibres were created for special features such as greater strength, stretch, colourfastness, wrinkle resistance, to prevent shrinkage or for easier care.

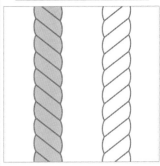

Top: *Grainlines and bias*
Bottom: *L to R: S-twist yarns,*
Z-twist yarns

YARN PLY AND TWIST

Fabrics are made from yarns that have a single strand of thread or multiple strands called ply. Usually, a higher ply equals a stronger or heavier-weight fabric. As the threads are twisted into yarns, they can be twisted clockwise or anti-clockwise. This is referred to as the type of twist; yarns are called Z twist or S twist. Yarns can be high twist or low twist – the number of rotations and the amount of twist affect the look and feel of a fabric. High-twist yarns tend to be smoother and stronger while low-twist yarns can pill since the fibres can pull apart.

WEAVES

Woven fabrics have different weave patterns. The three basic weaves types are plain, twill and satin weave. In plain-weave fabrics, one weft thread goes over one warp, under one warp, over one, under one, and so on. This is how most basic fabrics are made, including quilting cotton, taffeta, canvas and chiffon. Twill weaves have a noticeable diagonal and have the weft thread going over two warp threads, under two, over two, and so on. Twill-weave fabrics include denim, gabardine, herringbone and houndstooth. Twill weaves tend to have more drape than plain weaves. In satin-weave fabrics, the weft thread goes under three or more warp threads and over only one. They can also be made with the weft going over several warp threads and under one. Because of these long floats of threads, satin-weave fabrics reflect light and are very smooth, but tend to snag. Common satin-weave fabrics include satin, charmeuse and sateen. Fabrics can be woven with a single colour or multiple colour threads to create yarn dyes such as plaids and stripes.

Top: *Plain weave*
Middle: *Twill weave*
Bottom: *Satin weave*

WIDTH

Fabrics are made in different widths and they are measured from selvage to selvage. The two most common widths are 112/114cm (44/45in) wide and 147/152cm (58/60in) wide. The smaller number is the measurement of usable fabric and the bigger number includes the selvage. Fabric is sold by the length, so one metre of a 112/114cm fabric would be 91cm long by 114cmwide (36in by 45in) wide. You cannot buy a partial width but you can buy a fraction of a metre.

LOOPED AND PILE FABRICS

Some fabrics have a looped or raised surface of threads. Velvets, velveteen, faux furs and corduroy are examples of fabrics with a pile (or nap) and the fibres have a direction, so all pieces should be cut with the fibres pointing down. Other fabrics, such as terry cloth, have a looped pile that may or may not have a direction.

FINISHES

Once a fabric is woven or knitted, it can have a finish applied to the surface. Fabrics can be dyed, printed, embossed or embroidered. They can be brushed to make the surface very soft. The surface of the fabric can be coated or glazed to make it shiny or water resistant. And some fabrics are treated with chemicals to make them stain resistant.

1 METRE OF 112/114cm (44/45in) WIDE FABRIC
114cm (45in) WIDE INCLUDING
EACH 1.3cm (½in) SELVAGE
112cm (44in) WIDE USABLE FABRIC
91cm (36in) LONG

1.3cm SELVAGE

1.3cm SELVAGE

Top: *How a metre of fabric measures out*

Common fabrics

What makes a particular type of fabric is its unique combination of fibre, weave, weight, colour, pattern, print and finish. Here is a list of common fabrics and their characteristics.

1. **Batiste:** very lightweight and sheer plain-weave cotton, synthetic or a blend.

2. **Broadcloth:** medium-weight plain-weave cotton, synthetic or a blend. Can be solid or printed and is the base cloth for most quilting cottons.

3. **Burlap:** loosely woven plain-weave fabric made from jute, with a rough, ropelike texture. Traditionally tan but also available in other solid colours.

4. **Canvas:** heavyweight plain-weave fabric in cotton, synthetic or a blend. Often the base for home décor fabrics.

5. **Charmeuse:** lightweight and drapey satin-weave fabric used for dressy garments or lingerie. Can be silk, synthetic, or a blend.

6. **Chiffon:** lightweight, drapey and transparent plain-weave fabric made from both S-twist and Z-twist yarns that create a crêpe texture. Can be silk, cotton, synthetic or a blend. Often printed.

7. **China silk:** extremely lightweight plain-weave silk used for linings and lingerie.

8. **Coating:** heavyweight fabrics made of wool, wool blend or other hair fibres to make outerwear. Can be solid or yarn dyes and can be brushed for softness.

9. **Corduroy:** plain-weave or twill-weave cotton or cotton-blend fabric with a pile and noticeable vertical ribs called wales. Can be wide-wale or pinwale and is measured in wales per inch.

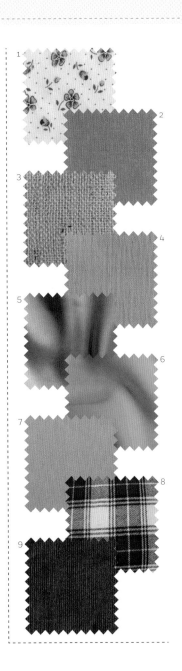

10. **Denim:** medium- to heavyweight twill-weave cotton or cotton blend with blue warp threads and white weft threads.

11. **Dotted Swiss:** lightweight and sheer plain-weave cotton with woven-in dots. Imitation Dotted Swiss has printed or flocked dots.

12. **Eyelet:** cotton plain-weave fabric with embroidery around openwork holes.

13. **Felt:** non-woven fabric made by pressing and matting fibres together with heat, steam and pressure. Can be wool, synthetic or a blend.

14. **Flannel:** plain-weave fabric with a brushed surface in light to medium-weight. Can be wool, wool blend or cotton.

15. **Gabardine:** basic twill-weave fabric made in any fibre. Comes in a variety of weights and is usually solid.

16. **Gingham:** plain-weave fabric made with two evenly alternating coloured threads in both the warp and weft to form the recognisable checkerboard.

17. **Herringbone:** twill-weave fabric where the twill weave diagonal alternates direction to produce a striped effect. Can be woven with a single colour or with two colours. Usually wool or a wool blend and a medium- to heavyweight.

18. **Houndstooth:** twill-weave fabric woven with two evenly alternating colours in both the warp and weft to create a checked effect. Traditionally black and white, wool or a wool blend, and a medium- to heavyweight.

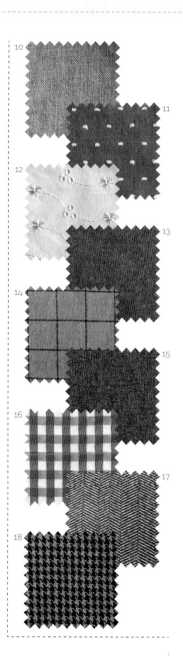

19. **Interlock:** knitted fabric that looks the same on both sides, has cut edges that don't curl, and stretch from 25 to 75 percent. Can be any fibre.

20. **Jersey:** knitted fabric that looks different on the reverse, has cut edges that curl towards the right side, and usually about 25 percent stretch. Can be any fibre.

21. **Lace:** can be knitted, woven, crocheted or knotted by hand or machine. Characterised by decorative openwork surface. Can be cotton, silk or synthetic fibres.

22. **Lawn:** lightweight, crisp and slightly sheer plain-weave cotton or cotton-blend fabric. Heavier than batiste and crisper than voile.

23. **Leather:** non-woven material made from animal hides. Ranges from very lightweight and soft to very heavy and stiff. Leather is sold by the hide and is irregularly shaped. Can be dyed, printed and embossed.

24. **Linen:** plain-weave and crisp fabric made from linen fibres. Characterised by its slubby surface and tendency to wrinkle. Ranges from very lightweight handkerchief linen to heavyweight suiting. Often blended with rayon or cotton for drape and wrinkle resistance. There are also 'linen-look' fabrics made from synthetics.

25. **Muslin:** plain-weave cotton fabric used for test garments and fitting.

26. **Organza:** tightly woven, crisp and sheer plain-weave silk or synthetic fabric used for evening wear.

27. **Plaid:** plain-weave fabric made with unevenly alternating coloured threads in both the warp and weft that form squares and stripes. Can be any fibre in any weight.

28. **Poplin:** medium-weight plain-weave cotton or cotton blend with a higher thread count and smoother surface than broadcloth.

29. **Ribbing:** knitted fabric constructed from alternating knit and purl stitches to create vertical ribs. It may look the same or different on the reverse, tends not to curl and has up to 100 percent stretch.

30. **Sateen:** smooth satin-weave fabric made of cotton or cotton blend. This medium- to heavyweight fabric is the base cloth for many home décor fabrics.

31. **Satin:** smooth satin-weave fabric made from silk, synthetics or blends. Lightweight to heavyweight and can have a shiny or matte surface.

32. **Seersucker:** cotton or cotton-blend plain-weave fabric with flat stripes alternating with coloured puckered stripes in the warp.

33. **Shantung:** plain-weave silk with a slubby surface made from silk threads that have slubs. Can also be a synthetic fibre and is usually solid.

34. **Taffeta:** smooth, crisp and opaque plain-weave fabric made from silk, synthetics or blends. Has a characteristic rustling sound. Used for evening wear and linings.

35. **Ticking:** very tightly woven twill-weave cotton fabric with a narrow two-tone yarn dye stripe. Traditionally used for pillows to prevent the quills of feathers and down from poking through.

36. **Tweed:** plain-weave wool with a rough texture and knotted surface. Usually yarn dyed with several different colours in both the warp and weft threads.

37. **Velvet:** dressy pile fabric made of silk, synthetic or blends. Has an extra set of warp yarns woven in and can range from lightweight to heavyweight.

38. **Velveteen:** casual pile fabric made of cotton, synthetic or blends. Has an extra set of weft yarns woven in and can range from lightweight to heavyweight.

39. **Voile:** lightweight, soft and slightly sheer plain-weave cotton or cotton-blend fabric. Heavier than batiste and softer than lawn.

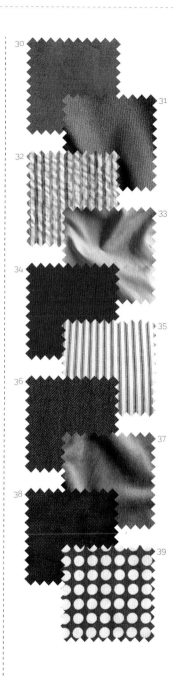

How to identify fabrics

Use the burn test to identify the fibre content of a mystery fabric. This will help you to sew, press and care for your project. Make sure to work in a ventilated area and place a non-flammable container under the burning swatch. Clip off a 8cm (3in) piece of the fabric, hold one end with sturdy metal tweezers and light one end of the sample. Observe the sample for the results listed here to determine the fibre content. If you think your fabric might be a blend of fibres, unravel the sample and burn the different yarns individually.

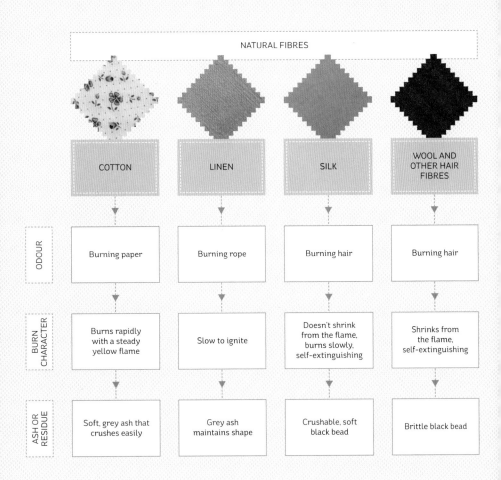

NATURAL FIBRES			
COTTON	LINEN	SILK	WOOL AND OTHER HAIR FIBRES
ODOUR			
Burning paper	Burning rope	Burning hair	Burning hair
BURN CHARACTER			
Burns rapidly with a steady yellow flame	Slow to ignite	Doesn't shrink from the flame, burns slowly, self-extinguishing	Shrinks from the flame, self-extinguishing
ASH OR RESIDUE			
Soft, grey ash that crushes easily	Grey ash maintains shape	Crushable, soft black bead	Brittle black bead

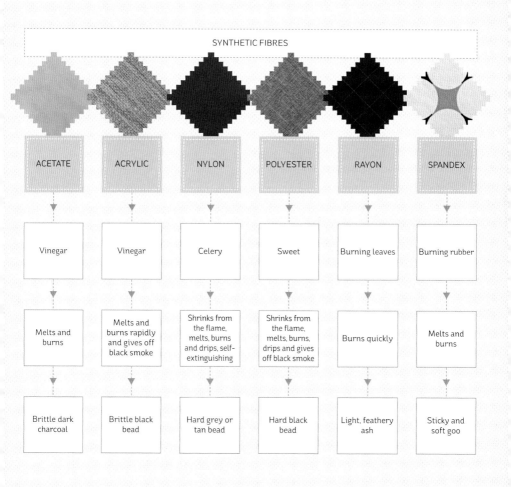

SYNTHETIC FIBRES

ACETATE	ACRYLIC	NYLON	POLYESTER	RAYON	SPANDEX
Vinegar	Vinegar	Celery	Sweet	Burning leaves	Burning rubber
Melts and burns	Melts and burns rapidly and gives off black smoke	Shrinks from the flame, melts, burns and drips, self-extinguishing	Shrinks from the flame, melts, burns, drips and gives off black smoke	Burns quickly	Melts and burns
Brittle dark charcoal	Brittle black bead	Hard grey or tan bead	Hard black bead	Light, feathery ash	Sticky and soft goo

Supporting materials

INTERFACING

Interfacing is a support material that stiffens, strengthens or stabilises another fabric. It is used in collars, cuffs, waistbands, lapels and plackets, and in handbags and home décor projects.

Types of interfacing

Interfacing can be woven, non-woven or even knit. It can be fusible and bonded to the wrong side of your fabric or it can be sew-in and stitched to the seam allowance of your fabric.

Every sewer should know

Interfacings come in all different degrees of thickness and stiffness so check the bolt for the correct type for your project and fabric.

LININGS

Linings go inside a garment and are used to hide seams, make the item more durable, more comfortable against the skin and more opaque.

Types of linings

Traditional lining fabrics are silk or synthetics such as Bemberg rayon, polyester or acetate. They come in solids and prints and in any weave and colour.

Top: Fusible interfacing

Bottom: Assorted lining fabrics

Every sewer should know

The choice of fabric for the lining depends on the type of project and the main fabric you are using. I like to line dresses in cotton lawn or voile because it is lightweight and breathable. For jackets that slide over another garment, you need something slippery so the fabrics don't catch on each other.

Q. WHAT IS THE DIFFERENCE BETWEEN INTERFACING AND INTERLINING?

A. Interlining is a layer of fabric that goes in between the fabric and the lining rather than being attached to the fabric.

Choosing the right fabric

The right fabric is the key to a successful project. Your fabric must work with the design elements of the garment or item. Here's a handy checklist to help you pick the right fabric:

Drape: for garments, how does the fabric drape on the body? Does it cling to the body's curves or stand away from the body? Use stiff fabrics for structured garments and garments that have architectural details such as pleats and use soft fabrics for garments with gentle gathers or that are cut on the bias. Soft fabrics can be given more structure with interfacings.

Difficulty of the fabric: don't use a tricky fabric on a complicated project! Save the difficult fabrics for simple projects and use the easy fabrics for more challenging designs.

Durability: does the fabric pill or fray? Everyday items should be made from fabrics that withstand lots of use and maintain their appearance.

Expense: for projects that need lots of metreage use low-priced fabric. Use high-quality fabrics on projects that require less metreage.

Hand: how does the fabric feel against your skin? Scratchy fabrics can be uncomfortable directly against the skin and are better for outerwear, or else they should be lined.

Plaids and prints: how does the scale of the plaid or print work with the design elements of the project? Will there be lots of seams to interrupt the print? Will you have to match the plaid or print across seam lines? That takes care and time when cutting. Is it a one-way print or napped fabric so that all the pattern pieces will have to be cut in one direction? That can take a lot more yardage.

Sheer fabrics: does it have to be lined or have special seam finishes? That will add time to a project.

TIP
Everyday items that get a lot of use should be as easy-care as possible while special-occasion items are fine for special washing or dry-cleaning only.

CHAPTER 6
PATTERN SOLUTIONS

Sewing patterns use many terms and symbols but once you understand them, you will realise that patterns are fairly universal. There are four large pattern companies, referred to as the Big 4: Butterick, McCall's, Simplicity and Vogue. Smaller companies include Kwik Sew and Burda, and there are also independent pattern companies. I often compare sewing patterns to cooking recipes. They have a materials list that is like your ingredients list and a sequence of steps that should be followed in the order given.

Pattern envelope translation

Both the front and back of a sewing-pattern envelope have important information to help you choose the right pattern and size.

FRONT

The front of the pattern envelope is likely to have the pattern company name, pattern number or name and a photograph or illustration of the styles included with the pattern. The front of the pattern envelope should also state the sizes that are included with the pattern. Most modern patterns are multi-sized but vintage patterns usually come with only one size.

Patterns can also be multi-view or single view. A multi-view pattern may contain several different garments or variations on the same garment, such as a skirt that has different lengths and waistbands. A single-view pattern has one option included.

BACK

First, check the size, scale and measurements for bust, waist and hips. The Big 4 pattern companies use consistent sizing between them while independents use their own individual size systems. Pattern sizes are often larger than ready-to-wear sizes so always check the measurements. For instance, I usually wear a size 8 or 10 in clothing but I am a 14 or 16 in patterns from the Big 4 and a 10 in Colette patterns.

Top: *Pattern envelope front*
Middle: *Pattern sizing*
Bottom: *Company name*

SIZE/ TAILLE	6	8	10	12	14	16	18	20	22	24
BUST	30½	31½	32½	34	36	38	40	42	44	46
WAIST	23	24	25	26½	28	30	32	34	37	39
HIP	32½	33½	34½	36	38	40	42	44	46	48
T. DE POITRINE	78	80	83	87	92	97	102	107	112	117
T. DE TAILLE	58	61	64	67	71	76	81	87	94	99
T. DE HANCHES	83	85	88	92	97	102	107	112	117	122

The back of the envelope has a technical drawing of the garment and a drawing of the back view so you can see details that may not have been apparent on the front illustration. For example, is there a centre back zip? Darts or gathers? The technical sketch is also usually drawn accurately in proportion. A description will give details about how fitted the style is and about closures, linings, and embellishments.

The metreage chart gives the amount of fabric you will need for your view and size, and for the width of the fabric you are using. Usually, patterns give metreage requirements for 114cm (45in)- and 152cm (60in)-wide fabrics, but what if you are using a 137cm (54in)-wide fabric? I usually go with the 114cm requirements to be safe, but take notes because I may be able to get away with less metreage in the future. The pattern may also indicate metreage requirements for fabrics with a nap and fabrics without a nap. Napped fabrics include prints with a one-way design and mean that all the pattern pieces need to point in one direction. This requires more fabric and therefore has a separate metreage requirement.

You should see a section that lists suggested fabrics. While you can certainly make a pattern in any fabric you like, the suggested fabrics all have a similar weight and drape that will sew up well in that style. Patterns for stretch knits will be marked as such, and knit and woven patterns are generally not interchangeable.

Some patterns list the number of pattern pieces. I always find this helpful because the more pattern pieces required, the longer the project will take to make. So if I want to make something fast, I look for styles that have four pieces or less. Fewer pattern pieces to cut equals less fabric to cut and sew.

Most patterns will also list any notions you will need. This includes items such as thread, zips (with length needed), buttons and snaps (number and size needed), ribbons and trims, elastics and more. Interfacing might be listed here or with fabric metreages.

Top: *Pattern envelope back*

Bottom: *Fabric and notion details*

SEE ALSO

page 80: *Common fabrics*

page 86: *Interfacing*

page 86: *Linings*

Pattern symbols and terms

Patterns are usually printed on large sheets of tissue paper, but some of the smaller independent pattern companies print their patterns on heavier bond paper. The tissue is very thin and delicate, so be careful when unfolding it. The pattern is sheer so you can see your fabric through it, which helps you to lay out fabrics with prints. Modern patterns are multi-sized, and all the sizes are nested together.

Now, let's move on to the pattern instructions.

1. First, you will see a group of technical sketches of the different views for both front and back views. Circle or highlight the view you are working on.

2. Next, you will see sketches of all the different pattern pieces included with the pattern and which view they each go with. Again, highlight the ones that go with your view.

3. You will have a key to the various symbols that might appear on the pattern as well as some sewing techniques. These tend to be the same for all the patterns that a company produces, so there might be some symbols listed that are not printed on your pattern.

4. Near the symbols should be explanations for what each one means. The most common ones you see are little diamonds for notches. Notches are used to match up pattern pieces together. Traditionally, you would find single notches to match up front pieces, double notches to match fronts to backs, and triple notches to match backs to each other. But I have seen some patterns that just use single notches.

You may also see dots, circles and squares. These are used to mark placements for zip stops, pockets, gathering and more. Parallel lines designate where patterns can be lengthened and shortened.

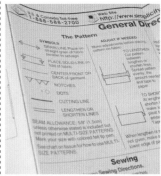

Top: *Multi-sized pattern*

Middle: *Sketches of the pattern pieces found in the pattern instructions*

Bottom: *Universal pattern symbols*

How To Use Your Multi-Size Pattern

First Prepare Your Pattern

Select the pattern pieces according to the view you are making. This pattern is made to body measurements with ease allowed for comfort and style. If your body measurements differ from those on the pattern envelope adjust the pieces before placing them on the fabric.

Check your back neck to waist and dress length; if necessary, alter the pattern. Lengthening and shortening lines are indicated.

1. **TO LENGTHEN:** Cut pattern between printed lines and place paper underneath. Spread pattern the required amount and pin to paper.

TO SHORTEN: Fold at the printed lines to form a pleat half the amount to be shortened, i.e. 1.3cm (½in) deep to shorten 2.5cm (1in).

Study Your Pattern Markings

2. **STRAIGHT GRAIN:** Place an even distance from selvage or a straight thread.
3. **FOLD:** Place on fold of fabric.
4. **LENGTHENING AND SHORTENING LINES.**
5. **SEAM ALLOWANCE:** 1.5cm (⅝in) unless otherwise stated.
6. **NOTCHES:** Match notches
7. **CUTTING LINES:** Multi patterns have different cutting lines for different sizes.
8. **TAILOR-TACKS:** With double thread make two loose stitches forming loop through fabric layers and pattern leaving long ends. Cut loop to remove pattern. Snip thread between fabric layers. Leave tufts.

Cutting layouts

Cutting Directions

FOR FOLDED AND DOUBLE LAYER FABRIC–Place fabric with right side inside and pin pattern on wrong side of fabric.

FOR SINGLE LAYER–Pin pattern on right side of fabric.

NOTE: Pattern pieces may interlock more closely for smaller sizes. Cut notches out from cutting line.

BEFORE removing pattern from fabric, transfer all pattern markings using tailor tacks or dressmaking tracing paper.

9. KEY: Pattern printed side down
10. KEY: Pattern printed side up
11. KEY: Cut out all pieces except pieces that extend beyond folded fabric, then open out fabric and cut in positions as shown.
12. KEY: For with and without nap layouts ensure fabric is placed with nap or design running in same direction. Before pinning to fabric, press tissue pattern with a warm dry iron to remove creases.

Sewing Directions

Fabric Key

Sew garment following Sewing Directions.
PIN or machine-baste seams matching notches.
STITCH 1.5cm (⅝in) seams unless otherwise stated.
PRESS seams open unless otherwise indicated, clipping when necessary so seams will lie flat.

EASE-STITCH or GATHER–Loosen needle tension slightly. With RIGHT side up, stitch 1.5cm (⅝in) from cut edge using a long stitch. Stitch again 6mm (¼in) away in the seam allowance.

EDGE FINISH – Neaten raw edges of seams, hems and facings using one of the following methods.

13. Stitch 6mm (¼in) from edge, turn under along stitching and stitch.
14. Zigzag or overlock raw edges.

INTERFACING–Pin interfacing to WRONG side of fabric. Cut across corners that will be enclosed with seams. Machine-baste 1.3cm (½in) from cut edge. (Shown only on first illustration). Trim interfacing close to machine-basting. For FUSIBLE interfacing, follow manufacturer's directions.

15. **STAY-STITCH**–Stitch 1.3cm (½in) from cut edge, in direction of arrows. (Shown only in the first illustration.)

LAYERING–Trim seam allowance in layers.

16. Layer enclosed seams
17. Trim corners
18. Clip inner curves
19. Notch outer curves
20. **UNDERSTITCH**–Press facing away from garment, press seam towards facing. Facing side up, understitch close to seam through facing and seam allowances.

You will see arrows to indicate grainline and bracketed arrows to indicate patterns that need to be placed against a fold. There might be markings to indicate button and buttonhole placements. There should also be an indication of which seam allowance your pattern is using. Most commercial patterns use 1.6cm (⅝in) seam allowance but some use 1.3cm (½in), 1cm (⅜in) or just 6mm (¼in) seam allowance.

5. Once you have cut out the correct size, iron the pattern to remove any wrinkles. A warm and dry iron is perfect for this since steam and paper are a bad combination. Snip your notches and punch open any dots, circles and squares.

6. Read through your pattern instructions to make sure you understand all the steps. I like to highlight the instructions that refer to the view I am making to ensure that I don't work off instructions for one of the other views. There is nothing more frustrating than getting halfway through and realising you have made a huge mistake and need to recut something. Patterns will often have the construction steps explained with both words and pictures.

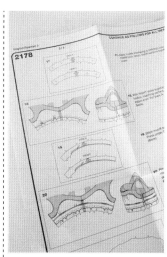

Top: *Illustrated pattern instructions*

Pattern and fabric layouts

Once you have cut out your pattern pieces and ironed them smooth, it is time to lay out your fabric. There should be a diagram showing how you need to do this. It is very rarely explained anywhere. First, find the layouts for the view you are making. Then look for a sketch showing the width of fabric you are using. There will be a diagram for 114cm (45in)-wide fabrics and possibly a different one for 152cm (60in)-wide fabrics. Notice that the 152cm-wide layout uses less fabric. If the layout is the same for both widths, then the sketch will indicate that it's for both. If I am using 137cm (54in) fabric, I tend to use the layout for 114cm-wide fabric but take notes to see if I can squeeze things in tighter to save myself metreage in the future. There might also be a separate layout for fabrics with a nap and fabric without a nap.

Most layouts are for a double layer of fabric and the sketch should look like a folded piece of fabric and indicate where the fold is (F) and where the selvages are lined up (S). The fabric should be folded with right sides together. But some layouts are just a single layer of fabric for asymmetrical or bias-cut pattern pieces.

You might come across a special layout where only one selvage is folded towards the centre to give you both a double layer and single layer.

Another special layout is where both selvages are folded in towards the centre. You see this on T-shirts and other styles that don't have front and back centre seams and need to be cut on the fold.

Once you find your correct layout, arrange your fabric as per the diagram and then place the pattern pieces according to the layout.

TIP

Tissue patterns can be difficult to work with since they are lightweight and tear easily. Iron fusible interfacing to the wrong side of your pattern pieces before you cut them out. It will make them heavier and easier to cut, and the interfacing will give the back of the pattern a bit of a 'tooth' so the pattern sticks to your fabric. Your patterns will also last much longer.

Top left: *Standard pattern layout*
Top right: *Single layer pattern layout*
Bottom left: *Double fold pattern layout*
Bottom right: *Half-fold pattern layout*

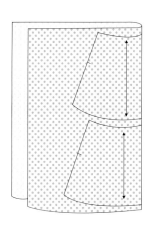

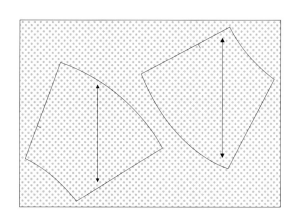

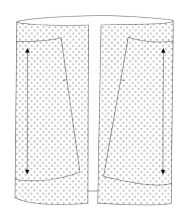

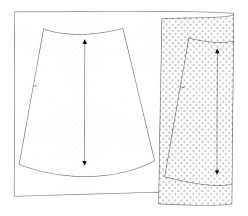

Cutting fabric

There are several different methods to secure your pattern to the
fabric and to cut out your fabric.

SECURING FABRIC: METHOD ONE

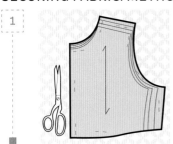

Traditionally, sewers would pin the pattern pieces to the
fabric around the edges. I am personally not a fan of this
technique because it tends to distort the fabric and is
time consuming.

SECURING FABRIC: METHOD TWO

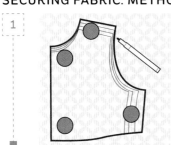

My favourite method is to weigh down my pattern pieces and
trace around the edges with a fabric marker or chalk. You can
use soup tins, flat washers from the hardware store, paper
weights or anything you happen to have around that's heavy.
Then once the pattern pieces are traced, remove the pattern
and you have a clearly visible line to cut on.

Now it's time to cut. You can either use scissors or a rotary
cutter and mat. The goal when cutting is to keep your fabric
flat to maintain accuracy. Don't lift and shift the fabric as you
cut! You should move; don't move the fabric.

CUTTING FABRIC: METHOD ONE

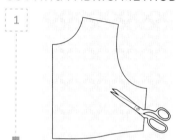

When using scissors, always keep the bottom blade of the scissors flat on the table. Don't lift the scissors and cut in the air because that will distort the fabric. Take long, smooth cuts rather than small, choppy ones. Long, smooth cuts are faster, more accurate, and less work for you!

CUTTING FABRIC: METHOD TWO

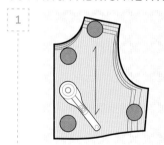

The other option is to use a rotary cutter and mat. Slide the cutting mat under the fabric and carefully cut around using the rotary cutter. Be extra careful at interior corners that you don't overcut. You might want to use scissors to snip those corners.

SEE ALSO
page 50: Tailor's chalk
page 51: Markers and pens
page 56: Cutting tools

Marking fabric

There are various ways to mark all those notches, dart lines and other design details.

1

The easiest way to mark notches is to clip into the seam allowance by 6mm (¼in). Use just the tip of your scissors to make sure you don't clip too far.

2

You can use a water-soluble or air-soluble fabric marker or tailor's chalk to draw in darts and pleats and to mark placement for buttonholes and buttons as well as zip stops and gathers. Just poke your pen through all those punched dots, circles and squares.

3

A great way to mark dots through multiple layers of fabric is to slide a pin through the hole and through all the layers. Then, layer by layer, mark where the pin comes through.

4

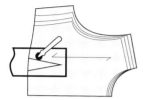

Lots of sewers use a tracing wheel and carbon paper, also known as dressmaker's transfer paper. The paper is available in several colours such as white, blue, yellow and red. Use the colour that will contrast best against your fabric. Place a piece against each wrong side of your fabric and then run the tracing wheel on the seam lines on the pattern.

When your remove the pattern piece and transfer paper, you should see a dotted line.

5

If you're afraid that pen or chalk marks will disappear by the time you need them, then you can use thread to mark design details. Thread tracing works well for lines and tailor tacks work well for dots. To thread trace, thread a needle with a contrasting thread and stitch long basting stitches along the dart legs and pleat lines.

6

Tailor tacks are little loops of thread. Thread your needle with a double strand of thread and stitch through the pattern and both layers of fabric at your marks. Separate the layers and clip through, leaving long thread tails.

SEE ALSO

page 22: *Handsewing needles*
page 28: *Threads*
page 50: *Tailor's chalk*
page 51: *Markers and pens*
page 52: *Tracing wheels*
page 53: *Transfer paper*

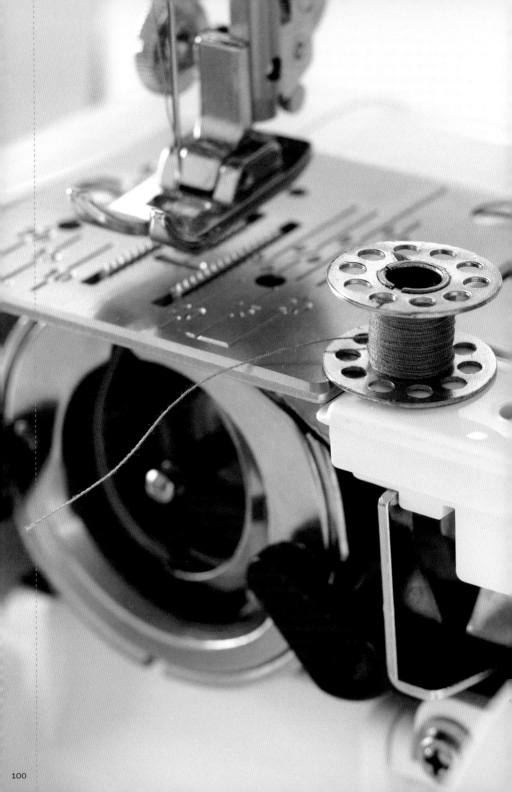

CHAPTER 7
SEWING SOLUTIONS

It's important to understand sewing fundamentals such as correct machine threading, straight seams, seam allowances and basic stitches to ensure trouble-free and happy sewing. Then add on some intermediate skills such as corners, curves, darts and pressing, and you are set for nearly any project.

Machine basics

TIP

You may not want to completely fill a bobbin for a small project such as a pillow, but always fill it for big projects. In fact, fill two so that you have a backup bobbin ready to go.

WINDING BOBBINS

Bobbins do not come with thread on them so you need to wind thread on. Never wind more thread on to a bobbin that already has thread on it or you will cause thread jams.

1 Place your spool of thread on the spool pin and pull the thread through the mini tension discs. It must go between the discs, not just around them.

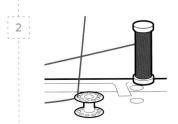

2 Take an empty bobbin and poke the thread up and out and through the top hole. If you are using a bobbin with many holes, pick your favourite.

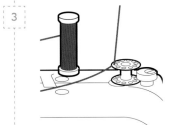

3 Place the bobbin on the bobbin winder and engage the winder by pushing it towards the stopper. On some machines, you engage by pushing the stopper towards the winder.

4

If necessary, manually disengage the needle and feed dog by pulling the handwheel out. Most computerised machines do this automatically when the bobbin winder is engaged.

TIP

Your sewing machine manual can answer many questions about your specific brand and model of sewing machine. You can order a replacement manual if you have lost yours. Order from the manufacturer's website or download a PDF version from sewusa.com.

5

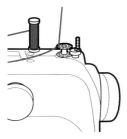

Hold the thread straight up and press the foot pedal to wind approximately a dozen rotations.

6

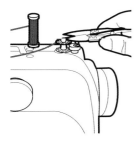

Make sure that the thread is winding smoothly, cut off the thread tail coming out of the hole, and continue winding to fill the bobbin. Most machines stop winding when the bobbin is full.

SEE ALSO

Chapter 1: The basic sewing machine

THREADING THE MACHINE

All sewing machines thread in the same sequence of steps. I always compare sewing machines to cars. If you drive and you rent a car, you can drive it, no matter the make or model. It's the same with sewing machines. Things might look a little different and be in slightly different places, but the parts and steps are the same.

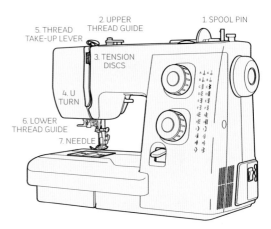

2. UPPER THREAD GUIDE
1. SPOOL PIN
5. THREAD TAKE-UP LEVER
3. TENSION DISCS
4. U TURN
6. LOWER THREAD GUIDE
7. NEEDLE

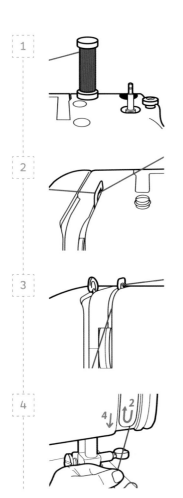

1

Spool pin
For vertical spool pins, the thread should pull from behind and to the left. For horizontal spool pins, the thread pulls from behind and under to the front. Place the thread on the spool pin and replace the spool cap.

2

Upper thread guide
There is usually only one but sometimes there can be several. Make sure you thread through all of them.

3

Tension discs
Pull the thread between the tension discs.

4

U turn
Pull the thread around the U turn and straight up. It should catch the little wire spring on the left side.

5

Thread take-up lever

Pull the thread through the take-up lever from right to left. You should pull it behind the lever and then all the way forwards to ensure that it lies in the eye.

6

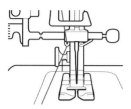

Lower thread guide

All sewing machines have a thread guide right above the needle. This prevents the thread from entering the needle eye on a sharp diagonal and keeps the stitches even. Some machines may have additional lower guides and if so, pull the thread through these as well.

7

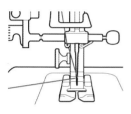

Needle

Always thread the needle front to back. To make threading easier, use a short length of thread. It's stiffer and easier to get through the needle. DO NOT lick the thread. That will introduce moisture into your sewing machine. Instead, trim the thread with thread snips. Hold the thread out front with your finger while pulling it through the needle to prevent the thread from wrapping around the needle.

8

Load the bobbin

For top-load bobbins, make sure the thread pulls off the bobbin in the shape of a letter P, drop the bobbin into the bobbin case and thread through the bobbin case.

For front-load bobbins, remove the bobbin case from the machine and, with the bobbin case open and facing you, drop the bobbin in the case in the shape of a number 9 and thread through the bobbin case. Insert the bobbin case in the machine, making sure it locks in place with the finger in the notch.

9

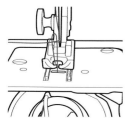

Pull up the bobbin thread

Hold on to only the top thread with your left hand and turn the handwheel towards you with your right hand. When both the needle and take-up lever are back up in the highest position, pull up on the top thread to raise a loop of the bobbin thread through the needle hole. Pull the bobbin thread up and free and pull both threads under the presser foot and towards the back of the machine.

TENSION

What is it and what does it do? Basically, the tension discs are two metal discs that are side by side and act as a speed control for your top thread. The thread passes between the discs, and depending on if the discs are close together or further apart, they control how quickly the top thread moves through the machine.

For tighter tension, the discs are closer together and they slow the thread down. For looser tension, the discs are further apart and the top thread can move more quickly through the machine. Generally, you want balanced tension, meaning that there is an equal amount of top thread and bobbin thread and the threads interlock in between the layers of fabric.

Most tension dials go from 0 to 9 with 4 being the default for balanced tension. Lower numbers equal looser tension and higher numbers equal tighter tension. You might want looser tension for a thicker thread such as topstitch thread or a tighter tension for thinner threads. Always have the presser foot UP for threading because that disengages the tension discs and allows the thread between the discs.

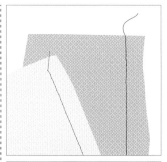

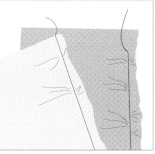

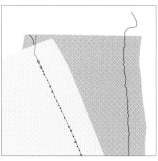

Top: *Balanced tension*
Middle: *Tension that is too tight*
Bottom: *Tension that is too loose*

TIP

You can also adjust your bobbin tension. So if you still think there's a tension issue, check the bobbin tension. On the bobbin case there is a little screw that tightens the clamp. Sometimes, the little screw can loosen due to the vibrations of the machine.

CHANGING A NEEDLE

Needles are changed for one of three reasons:

1. If you break a needle.

2. When the needle is worn out or dull.

3. When you need a different type or size of needle.

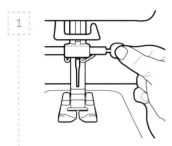

To remove the old needle, turn the screw above the needle clamp towards you a half turn and slide the needle down and out of the shaft. Make sure to dispose safely of old or broken needles.

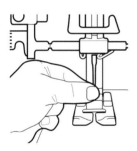

To insert a needle, make sure the flat side of the needle is towards the back, insert it into the shaft until it can't go up anymore, and tighten the screw.

SEE ALSO

page 24: Machine needles

TIP

Needles should be changed after every eight hours of sewing time or every three to four projects because needle tips wear down each time the needle penetrates the fabric. Dull needles cause skipped stitches.

TROUBLESHOOTING

If you are having issues with threads jamming and tangling or needles are breaking, check this handy list of common problems:

1. The machine is incorrectly threaded on the top or came unthreaded.

2. The bobbin is in backwards or the bobbin thread was never threaded through the bobbin case.

3. You are using the wrong type of bobbin or an incorrectly wound bobbin.

4. The needle is dull or bent, has been put in backwards or not pushed up all the way.

5. The machine is dirty and the threads are catching on lint.

6. The machine needs to be oiled.

7. You are using poor-quality thread.

8. The upper tension or lower tension needs to be adjusted.

Stitching basics

FEED DOG

The feed dog is the apparatus with little rows of teeth under the presser foot, which moves in an elliptical motion when the machine is operating. The teeth grip the bottom layer of fabric, the presser foot holds the fabric against the feed dog and the feed dog moves the fabric through the machine. You must have the presser foot down for sewing otherwise there is nothing holding the fabric against the feed dog and you will have a big, tangled mess. Your hands should not be pushing or pulling the fabric through the machine – your hands are for steering. Your right hand should be in front of the feed dog and resting lightly on the fabric to keep the layers smoothly feeding. Your left hand should be to the left of the presser foot and the feed dog, guiding the fabric.

SEAM ALLOWANCE

A seam is a row of stitching and the seam allowance is the distance from the seam to the edge of the fabric. This extra bit of fabric allows enough material to let out the seams for alterations. The standard seam allowance for patterns from the major pattern companies is 1.6cm (⅝in) but tight curves, such as necklines, often have a smaller seam allowance, for example, 1cm (⅜in). Many smaller pattern companies use 1.3cm (½in) seam allowances for all the seams. Commercial clothing uses 6mm (¼in) for knits (sewn on a serger) and 1cm (⅜in) for wovens. Smaller seam allowances save fabric and therefore money.

Top: *Feed dog*

Bottom: *Standard 1.6cm seam allowance*

TIP

It is crucial to follow the seam allowance in your pattern to ensure that the pattern fits correctly and the pieces match up.

SEAM GUIDES

On the needle plate of your sewing machine, there are markings to the right of the feed dog and presser foot. These are your seam guides. Each line is a measurement of the distance from the needle and most often the first line is 1cm (³⁄₈in), the second is 1.3cm (½in), the third is 1.6cm (⁵⁄₈in) and so on. Your machine may also be marked with a second set of lines marked 10, 15 and 20 – these are millimetres.

BACKSTITCHING

In handsewing, you tie a knot at the end of your thread to prevent your stitches from coming loose. In machine sewing, you should instead take three to five backstitches at the beginning and end of all of your seams to lock in the stitches. To backstitch, simply hold the reverse button in while pressing the foot pedal. The reverse button changes the direction of the feed dog so that it moves the fabric back towards you.

PINNING

Pins help keep your fabric layers aligned and even. Place the pins perpendicular to the seam and with the heads off the edge of the fabric so they are easy to see. I suggest one pin every 8 to 20cm (3in to 8in). You might want fewer pins for straight edges and stable fabrics and more for stretchy or slippery fabrics or for curves.

page 60: Pins

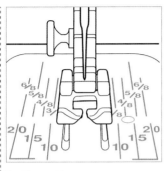

Top: *Seam guides*

TIP

Sometimes the seam guides can be difficult to see so you can add on an additional seam guide. There are magnetic seam guides that clamp on to the needle plate and seam guides that screw on. My favourite easy trick is to use blue painter's tape from the hardware store as a seam guide. It is very visible, repositionable and leaves no sticky residue.

TIP

Never sew over pins or you risk the needle hitting a pin and breaking, or even worse, the needle bending and pushing the pin down into the needle hole and seriously damaging your sewing machine. Always pull out the pins just before you get to them.

TIP

The secret to sewing straight seams is to NEVER watch the needle. Keep your eyes and fabric on the seam guide and your seam allowances will be even.

Sew slowly around curves and faster for straight seams.

SEWING A SEAM

The cardinal rule of sewing is right sides together and raw edges together. You sew inside out to hide the seam allowances when the fabrics are right sides out.

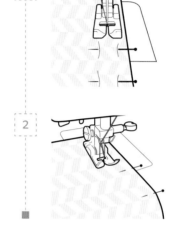

Lay your fabrics with the two right sides facing and line up the raw edges evenly. Align your fabric edges on the seam guide for your seam allowance. Then the needle will stitch the seam the correct distance from the edge.

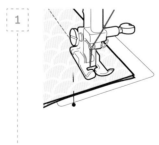

Always start and end your seams with the needle and take-up lever in the highest position. It's not necessary to manually lower the needle into the fabric before you press the foot pedal.

TIP

Never turn the handwheel away from you because that tends to jam and tangle the threads.

PIVOT TURNS

Pivot turns are used for sewing around corners and angles for things such as pockets and collars.

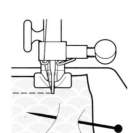

Sew your seam and when you get to 1.6cm (⁵⁄₈in) – or whatever seam allowance you are using – away from the end, stop and turn the handwheel towards you to sink the needle in the fabric. The needle will be your anchor.

Now you can safely lift the presser foot and pivot your fabric in the new direction.

Drop the presser foot back down and keep stitching. There is no need to backstitch because it's the same seam, just in a new direction.

SEE ALSO
page 126: Pockets

CLIPPING AND NOTCHING

Once you have stitched a seam, then you'll turn it right side out. But on curves and corners the seam allowances won't lay flat and tend to bunch up.

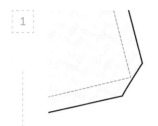

1 For exterior corners, cut off the seam allowance corner so that the remaining seam allowances can miter. Be very careful not to clip through the stitching. You want to clip up to the stitch line, stopping about 1mm (¹/₁₆in) away.

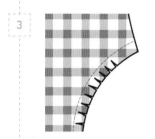

2 For interior corners, clip into the corner, stopping just short of the seam allowance.

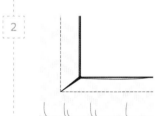

3 For concave curves, clip into the seam allowance stopping just short of the stitching. This will allow the seam allowance to spread.

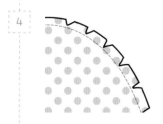

4 For convex curves, cut out little wedges or notches from the seam allowance to eliminate bunching and bulk.

TIP

You can clip corners and curves with your standard dressmaker's shears but it can be easier and you might have more control if you use small embroidery scissors.

SEE ALSO

page 56: Cutting tools
page 120: Opposing curves and easestitching

Basic stitches

Length and width

Stitch length controls the speed of the feed dog and is measured in millimetres from 0 to 4 (sometimes up to 6 for high-end machines). Higher numbers mean the feed dog moves faster in relation to the needle and the stitches are longer. The default setting is 2.5 mm. Stitch width controls how far away from the centre the needle can swing. A straight stitch has a width of 0mm, while a zigzag can be as narrow as 1mm or as wide as 4mm.

Straight stitch

You will use this for 99 percent of all your sewing. It is the basic construction stitch to connect one fabric to another. Use a 2.5-mm length for basic sewing, 4mm or longer for basting, 3mm for topstitching, and 1.5 to 2mm for stress points such as corners and purse straps. Straight stitches do not stretch so do not use them for stretch knits.

Zigzag

The zigzag can be used as a decorative topstitch, to finish seam allowances to prevent fabric edges from fraying, to sew on appliqués, stitch monograms and for sewing stretch knits. Use a 2.5-mm length and 3.5-mm width for basic sewing, 0.5-mm length and 4 to 5mm width for satin-stitching appliqués and embroidery, and a 2.5-mm length and 0.5-mm width for stretch sewing.

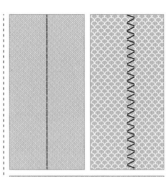

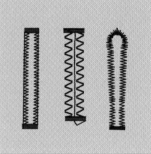

Top left: *Straight stitch*
Top right: *Zigzag stitch*
Bottom: *Standard buttonhole, knit buttonhole, keyhole buttonhole*

Buttonhole

A buttonhole is a box made of tiny zigzag stitches. You can stitch a buttonhole using the zigzag stitch, but it is easier to have a buttonhole stitch. Mechanical machines do a four-step buttonhole while computerised machines do an automatic or one-step buttonhole. Regular buttonholes are standard and can be used on all types of fabric and for all types of buttons. Keyhole buttonholes have a rounded end that opens wider for ball-type buttons. Knit buttonholes have a more defined zigzag stitch to allow for more stretch.

TIP

Note that mechanical machines can do only regular buttonholes.

SEE ALSO
page 170: *Buttonholes*

Tricot/elastic stitch

This stitch is also called the multi-stitch zigzag and is a zigzag stitch where each zig and zag is made of three straight stitches. It is used to attach elastic and stitch on knit fabrics. Since the stitches are smaller than a standard zigzag, there is less chance the stitches will snag but the stitch has lots of stretch.

Stretch straight

This stitch is a straight stitch with one stitch forwards, one back, and one forwards. This is a very strong stitch because it goes over the same spot three times and is often used for high-stress seams such as crotch seams. But it also can be used for knits – it has built-in stretch because the feed dog stretches the fabric slightly.

SEE ALSO
page 122: Sewing with knits

Overcasting

The overcast stitch resembles a serger stitch and uses both zigzag and straight stitches. It is used to finish the raw edges of fabric to prevent fraying.

SEE ALSO
page 116: Seam finishes

Blind hem

The blind hem has several tiny zigzags and then one large zigzag. It is used for hemming and is practically invisible from the right side.

SEE ALSO
page 20: Hem feet
page 162: Hems

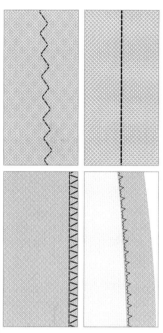

Top left: *Tricot/elastic stitch*
Top right: *Stretch straight stitch*
Bottom left: *Overcasting stitch*
Bottom right: *Blind hem stitch*

TIP

Computerised machines automatically adjust length and width for different stitches but you need to adjust manually on mechanical machines. On computerised machines, you can always change the settings from the default setting. Never adjust the width or stitch while the needle is in the fabric or you risk dragging the needle through the fabric and breaking it.

The importance of pressing

Pressing is one of the most important and underrated parts of sewing. As a general rule, you should press each seam right after you stitch it. You can have an item that is perfectly sewn but if the seams are not pressed well, they will look puckered and you will have a difficult time matching and stitching subsequent seams. You can camouflage an imperfect sewing job with an excellent pressing job. There is a difference between ironing and pressing. Ironing is sliding the iron across the surface of fabric to remove wrinkles. Pressing is holding the iron in one place to allow heat to penetrate and is used when applying fusibles, and when pressing seams and darts.

PRESSING TOOLS

Buy a good-quality steam iron with a range of temperatures that are clearly marked for different types of fabric. You don't want a poor-quality iron that is going to leak water and damage your fabric. You need a stable padded ironing board with adjustable height so that you can iron comfortably. In addition to an iron and ironing board, there are several other tools that make pressing seams and garments easier and faster, which are described below.

Sleeveboard

This looks like a miniature ironing board and is used for tight spaces or narrow items such as sleeves or pant legs.

Tailor's ham

This resembles a canned ham and is used for pressing curved seams without distorting them. One side is covered in wool to hold steam longer and the other is covered in cotton.

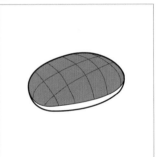

Top: *Sleeveboard*
Bottom: *Tailor's ham*

Press cloths

These can be made out of any fabric but are typically white muslin and about 30 by 46cm (12in by 18in) in size. They are used between an iron and the right side of your fabric and prevent scorching and shine marks.

TEMPERATURE AND STEAM

Different temperatures work best for different fibre contents. Linen and cotton need a high temperature to remove wrinkles and set seams while synthetics such as acrylic and acetate need a lower temperature or else they will melt. In addition to heat, some fabrics require a little steam. Follow the temperature guidelines on your iron but it's a good idea to iron a test swatch of the fabric first to avoid mistakes.

SEE ALSO

page 118: Darts, gathers and pleats
page 120: Opposing curves and easestitching

TIP

Use distilled water in your iron to prevent mineral deposits from discolouring and staining your fabrics.

Seam finishes

Once you have sewn a seam, you need to finish the raw
edges or they will start to fray, look messy and compromise
the integrity of your seams. Seam finishes should not be
visible from the right side so some methods will be better
for certain fabrics.

Pinking

This is probably the simplest method. Once you have stitched
the seam, use pinking shears to trim away 3mm (⅛in) of fabric.
Press the seam allowances open. This is a good solution
for tightly woven fabrics but it may still allow fraying on
loose weaves.

> **SEE ALSO**
> **page 56:** Cutting tools

Serging

If you have a serger, you can serge the raw edges and they will
not fray. If the seams are to be pressed open, then serge each
seam allowance separately. If they are going to be pressed
towards one side, then you could serge them together. The
serger knives will also trim away any stray threads, making for
a very neat and tidy edge. This is a good solution for nearly all
fabrics except sheer ones.

> **SEE ALSO**
> **page 16:** The serger/overlock machine

Overcast/zigzag

If you do not have a serger, you can achieve a very similar
effect using a zigzag or overcast stitch and an overcasting
foot. You will not have the serger knives to cut away any frays
but you can trim those afterwards with thread snips. This
works well for all but sheer fabrics.

> **SEE ALSO**
> **page 20:** Seam finishing feet
> **page 112:** Basic stitches

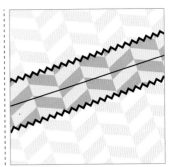
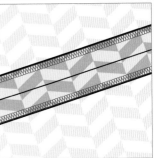
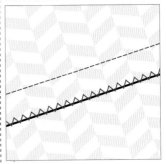

Top: *Pinked seam finish*
Middle: *Serged seam finish*
Bottom: *Zigzag seam finish*

Clean finish

Turn under the raw edges of each seam allowance about 3 to 6mm (⅛in to ¼in) and iron. Stitch close to the fold through the seam allowance only. This works for nearly all fabrics except bulky ones.

Bound

A bound finish (sometimes called a Hong Kong finish) encloses the raw edge of the seam allowance with another fabric. You can use purchased double-fold bias tape or make your own, but it should be from a thin fabric. This is an excellent option for bulky fabrics and unlined jackets.

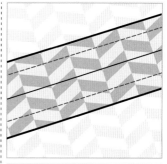

SEE ALSO
page 128: Making bias tape

French seam

This self-enclosed seam sounds fancy but is really simple. Start by sewing your seam WRONG sides facing with only a 1cm (⅜in) allowance. Trim away the excess leaving 3mm (⅛in) and press to one side. Now fold back so that right sides are facing and stitch a 6mm (¼in) seam – for a total of 1.6cm (⅝in). This seam is perfect for sheer fabrics but does not work for bulky fabrics or for tight curves.

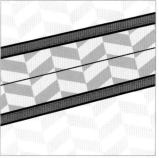

TIP

Finish the seam allowances AFTER you sew the seam. If you finish your raw edges before sewing your seam, it could change your seam allowance. A rule of thumb is stitch and then finish. If the item is going to be lined, then you could leave the edges raw because they will be protected by the lining. Knits can be left raw because knitted fabrics do not fray.

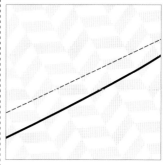

Top: *Clean seam finish*
Middle: *Bound seam finish*
Bottom: *French seam*

Darts, gathers and pleats

Darts, gathers and pleats all add shaping and allow a flat piece of fabric to mould around the contours of the body. Darts remove fullness and mould the fabric smoothly. They can be single pointed or double pointed and always point towards the fullest parts of the body. Gathers give soft, rounded shaping and add fullness. They look drapey in soft fabrics and poufy in stiff fabrics. Pleats create tailored shaping and add controlled fullness. Darts, gathers and pleats are interchangeable because each of them takes in fabric at a smaller part of the body. You can change a dart to gathers for a softer look. You can change gathers to pleats for a more tailored look.

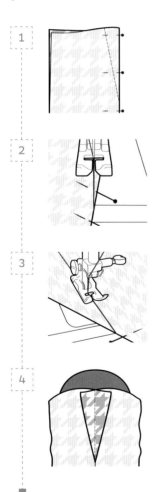

1

Darts

Mark your dart following the pattern markings using tailor's chalk, fabric marker or other method. Fold the dart right sides facing along the fold line and pin in place.

2

Always sew from the widest part towards the point. Backstitch at the wide point but don't backstitch at the point or you'll create a pucker. Instead, when you are approximately 1.3cm (½in) from the point, shorten your stitch length to 1mm and take the last couple of stitches right on the fold. Stitch off the edge and hand tie off the thread tails.

3

For double-pointed darts, stitch in two segments. Start by backstitching at the widest point and stitch towards one point in the same manner as for a single-pointed dart. Then stitch the other end from the widest point towards the other point.

4

Press vertical darts towards the centre and press horizontal darts down. You may find it helpful to press on top of a tailor's ham when pressing to maintain the shape. If you are using a thick fabric, you can slash the darts down the centre and press them open to reduce bulk.

SEE ALSO
page 98: *Marking fabric*
page 114: *Tailor's ham*

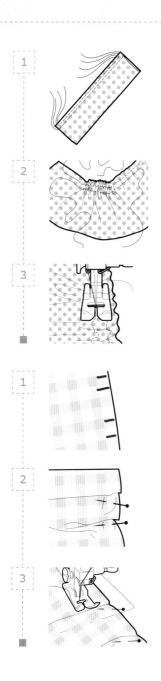

Gathers

Mark your beginning and ending gathering markings. Lengthen your stitch length to 4mm and loosen your upper tension to 0. Without backstitching at either end, stitch a row of basting stitches just inside the seam line. Baste another row 6mm (¼in) in from the seam line.

Pull on the bobbin threads to draw up the fabric by the desired amount.

Reset stitch length back to 2.5mm and tension back to 4, and stitch across the gathers just inside the seam line to secure them.

Pleats

Mark your pleat following the pattern markings using tailor's chalk, fabric marker or other method.

Fold the pleat along the fold line, align the fold with the placement line, and pin in place.

Stitch across the fold just inside the seam line to secure the pleat.

Press the pleats down the fold to create the desired amount of crispness.

Opposing curves and easestitching

Sometimes you have to sew a concave curve to a convex curve such as on princess seams. You have to stitch straight edges to curved edges when sewing collars to necklines. And sometimes you have to ease a slightly longer edge to a shorter edge when sewing sleeves into armholes. In each case, the seam lines match but the fabric edges do not, so markings and notches become crucial.

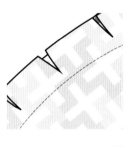

Opposing curves

With a standard straight stitch, stitch just inside the seam line of the concave curved piece to staystitch the seam and prevent it from stretching. Clip into the seam allowance to just short of the staystitching to allow the edge to spread to match the convex curve.

Match all markings and notches and pin the two pieces together with right sides facing. Stitch together with the clipped side on top.

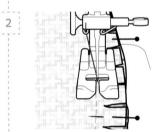

Cut notches in the seam allowance on the convex curve to reduce bulk and allow the seam allowance to lay flat.

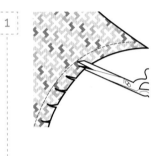

Place over a tailor's ham and press open the seam allowances. Turn right side out and press again.

SEE ALSO
page 111: Clipping and notching
page 114: Tailor's ham

Stitching a curved edge to a straight edge

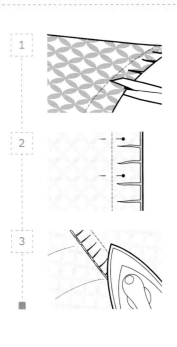

1 With a standard straight stitch, stitch just inside the seam line of the curved piece to staystitch the seam and prevent it from stretching. Clip into the seam allowance to just short of the staystitching to allow it to spread to match the straight edge.

2 Match all markings and notches and pin the two pieces together with right sides facing. Stitch together with the clipped side on top.

3 Press the seam allowances towards the straight piece. Turn right side out and press again.

SEE ALSO >
page 111: *Clipping and notching*

Easestitching

1 Mark your beginning and ending gathering markings on the piece to be eased. Lengthen your stitch length to 4mm. Without backstitching at either end, stitch a row of basting stitches just inside the seam line. Then baste another row 6mm (¼in) in from the seam line.

2 Pull on the bobbin threads to draw up the fabric the desired amount. Match all markings and notches and pin the two pieces together with right sides facing. Baste together with the clipped side on top. Check for any gathers or puckers. If there are any, rip out the stitches and try again. Only the seam allowance gathers; the seam lines should match smoothly.

3 Reset stitch length back to 2.5mm and stitch the two pieces together right on top of the basting stitches. Remove the basting stitches and press the seam allowances according to the pattern. Turn right side out and press again.

Sewing with knits

When constructing knit garments, the seams must stretch with the fabric so that the stitching will not break as you bend and move in the garment. While knit fabrics can be a little tricky to sew, the benefit is that fitting is much easier because of all that stretch and since knits don't fray, the seam allowances can be left unfinished.

Cutting

Many knit fabrics shift and curl, which can make cutting difficult. Therefore it's best to either weigh and trace your patterns and then cut with scissors or weigh and cut with a rotary cutter. Don't pin your pattern pieces because you will stretch and distort the fabric. If the fabric curling is extreme, try using spray starch to stabilise it.

SEE ALSO
page 96: *Cutting fabric*
page 98: *Marking fabric*

Stitches

Stitches that stretch are zigzag, stretch straight, stretch stitches and serger. Always do a test stitch on your fabric to see which works best because all knits have different degrees of stretch.

SEE ALSO
page 112: *Basic stitches*

Thread

When sewing knits, make sure to use a thread that has a bit of give, such as all-purpose polyester. Do not use 100-percent cotton because it has no give and will break.

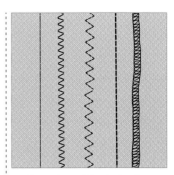

L to R: straight stitch (not for knits), zigzag stitch, elastic/tricot stitch, stretch straight stitch, serger stitch

TIPS

The wider the zigzag, the more stretch it will have. Always do a test stitch to make sure your stitch has enough stretch for that particular knit fabric.

Every knit fabric is different. Knit fabrics come in many different widths, including 114cm (45in), 122cm (48in), 132cm (52in), 140cm (55in) and even 178cm (70in) wide. This can make fabric layouts tricky. Follow your pattern but also try your own layout and see if you can fit the pieces in better, especially if you are using a wide fabric.

Needle types for knits

When you sew woven fabrics, the needle cuts a hole when it penetrates the fabric. But if you cut a hole through a knit fabric, then the fabric would start to unravel. So when you sew knits, you need to use a ballpoint needle. Rather than cutting a hole, the needle will push its way through the loops. Think of it like poking your finger through a loosely knitted sweater. Ballpoint/jersey needles are designed for basic knit fabrics while a stretch needle has a specially shaped scarf on the back for tightly knitted fabrics or fabrics with lots of spandex. Use these if a ballpoint needle is causing skipped stitches.

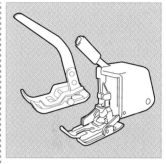

L–R: knit foot, even-feed/walking foot

SEE ALSO >·

***page 24:** Machine needles*

Feet

You can sew knits with a standard presser foot but sometimes the pressure of the presser foot can stretch out the fabric and cause rippling. Both a knit foot and a walking foot ensure that the two layers of fabric move evenly without rippling.

Fitting and finishing

Knitted garments often have negative ease, meaning that the garment is smaller than the body and will stretch to fit it. You will not need fitting seams such as darts as you do with wovens but you might have gathers and tucks to add fullness. Instead of zips and buttons, the garments can be pulled on and you can use elastic to finish waists, sleeves and necklines. You might leave hems raw, serged or rolled. You could also finish them with a band or a turn-back hem.

SEE ALSO >·

***Chapter 9:** Fitting solutions*

CHAPTER 8
EMBELLISHMENT
AND TRIMMING
SOLUTIONS

Sometimes a project needs a little something to really bring it to life. Pockets in contrasting fabrics can be decorative and are also practical and useful. Trims and appliqués are easy to attach and are a great way to customise your design!

Pockets

YOU WILL NEED:

- Fabric marker or tailor's chalk
- Clear ruler
- Scissors or rotary cutter and cutting mat
- Pins
- Iron and ironing board

TIP

You can use this method to make any shape of pocket: squares, rectangles, octagons, ovals... you name it! If you are going to make several pockets that are all the same, then make a template using pattern paper.

SEE ALSO

Chapter 3: *Marking, measuring and cutting tools*
page 116: *Seam finishes*

PATCH POCKETS: UNLINED

1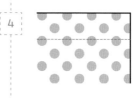

Figure out the finished pocket size and shape that you want and draw it on the wrong side of your fabric using your marker or chalk and ruler. Add 2.5cm (1in) for a facing at the top and then add a 1.3cm (½in) seam allowance all around the other sides. Cut out.

2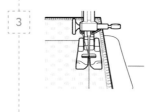

Finish all the edges by pinking, serging, overcasting or a clean finish.

3

Fold the top facing over so that the right sides are facing and pin in place. Staystitch along the seam lines on the sides and bottom.

4

Turn the pocket right side out and press the seam allowances towards the wrong side along the staystitch lines.

5

Topstitch the facing in place. Pin the pocket in place on to the item and edgestitch along the sides and bottom edges.

PATCH POCKETS: SELF-LINED

1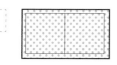

Figure out the finished pocket size you want and draw it on the wrong side of your fabric using your ruler and marker or chalk. I am making a 15cm (6in) pocket.

2 Draw another one right above it. Add a 1.3cm (½in) seam allowance all the way around. I now have a rectangle that is 18cm (7in) wide and 33cm (13in) high.

3

Cut out the shape.

4

Fold in half with right sides facing and pin in place. Stitch around the three sides with a 1.3cm (½in) seam allowance leaving a 8cm (3in) opening on the bottom.

5 Clip the corners and turn right side out.

6 Push out the corners using a point turner and press flat with the iron.

7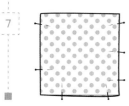

Pin the pocket in place on to the item and edgestitch in place along the sides and bottom edges. The fold will be the top edge of the pocket and is a very clean and neat edge.

YOU WILL NEED:

- Fabric marker or tailor's chalk
- Clear ruler
- Scissors or rotary cutter and cutting mat
- Pins
- Point turner
- Iron and ironing board

TIP

Use pins that are a different colour to mark the opening to remind you to leave it open.

SEE ALSO

Chapter 3: Marking, measuring and cutting tools
page 111: Clipping and notching

Bias tape

YOU WILL NEED:

- 46cm (½yd) of 114cm (45in) wide fabric – this will make about 8.2m (9yds) of a 5cm (2in) wide bias strip
- Tailor's chalk or fabric marker
- Clear ruler
- Pins
- Iron
- Scissors or rotary cutter and cutting mat

TIP

Fabrics with small prints work best because large prints might not be obvious on a narrow bias tape. Polka dots, stripes, ginghams, small florals and geometrics all look great! Note that 100 percent cottons press beautifully while synthetics and blends can be difficult to press well.

SEE ALSO

Chapter 3: Marking, measuring and cutting tools
page 76: *Grainlines and bias*

HOW TO MAKE A CONTINUOUS BIAS STRIP

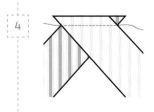

1 Fold the selvage over to form a triangle, creating a 45-degree fold along the bias. Cut along that fold and you have a bias-cut edge!

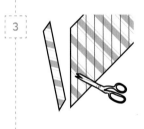

2 Pin the triangle to the other selvage with right sides facing and stitch with a 2.5cm (1in) seam allowance. Trim the seam allowances to 1.3cm (¼in), press the seam allowances open and you have a parallelogram.

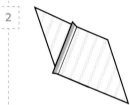

3 Decide how wide your strips should be. Your bias-tape maker should have instructions telling you how wide the strips need to be cut for each finished width of bias tape. Using your ruler and chalk, mark lines parallel to the bias edge across the entire piece of fabric. Cut apart on the lines.

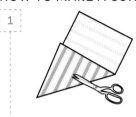

4 Now sew all the strips together. Take two strips of fabric that have edges angled in the same direction. Put with right sides together. You need the tip of each strip to overhang by 6mm (¼in) so they make a 90-degree angle with each other. Pin and stitch with a 6mm (¼in) seam allowance. Repeat until all the pieces are stitched and you have one long piece. Press the seam allowances open.

HOW TO USE A MANUAL BIAS-TAPE MAKER

1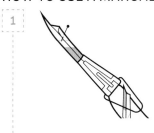

Insert the bias strip, wrong side up, into the wide end of the bias-tape maker. Pull through to the small end using a pin to help to guide it through. Pin the end to the ironing board to hold it in place.

2

Start pulling the bias-tape maker by the handle. As you pull through, you will see the edges fold over towards the middle. Press the folds as you gently pull the bias-tape maker. Go slowly and take care when pulling over the seams.

3

To make double-fold bias tape, fold in half with wrong sides facing and one side a bit wider than the other. Press in place.

YOU WILL NEED:

- Continuous bias strip
- Manual bias-tape maker
- Pin
- Iron
- Ironing board

TIP

When working with 100-percent cotton fabrics, a steam iron is necessary to achieve sharp folds. If you are using synthetics or blends, make sure to adjust the iron temperature accordingly.

SEE ALSO

page 34: Bias tape
page 66: Bias-tape makers: manual

YOU WILL NEED:

- Continuous bias strip
- Bias tape-making machine

TIP

The machine only makes single-fold bias tape. If you want double-fold bias tape, you can fold it in half and iron it. Bias tape-making machines come with a tip to make 2.5cm (1in) single-fold bias tape. Other sizes are sold separately.

HOW TO USE A BIAS TAPE-MAKING MACHINE

1 Open the machine, remove the bias tip and the ironing cover, assemble the guide bar, and remove the winding wheel. Wind the bias strip on the wheel with the right side facing out and reattach the winding wheel.

2 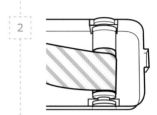 Lay the strip over the guide bar and pull the end of the strip through the bias tip. Re-attach the tip and pull the strip across the ironing plate. Re-attach the ironing plate cover.

3 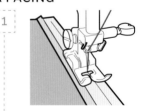 Plug in the machine, turn it on and set to the correct temperature for your fabric. When the machine is heated up, the READY button will light up. Press the RUN button and watch as the machine feeds the tape through and presses the folds in place.

YOU WILL NEED:

- Single-fold bias tape (either ready-made or handmade)
- Pins
- Iron and ironing board

TIP

In Step 1, I find it helpful to line up the crease in the centre notch of the presser foot and use that as my seam guide.

SEE ALSO ·

page 34: Bias tape
page 71: Bias tape-making machines
page 128: How to make a continuous bias strip

HOW TO ATTACH SINGLE-FOLD BIAS TAPE AS A FACING

1 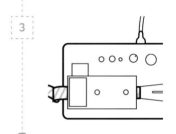 Lay the bias tape face down against the right side of the fabric it will be sewn to. Unfold the right edge so that the edges of the bias tape and the item are aligned and pin in place. Stitch in the crease.

2 Fold the bias tape over to the wrong side of the item to encase the raw edges and press in place with an iron.

3 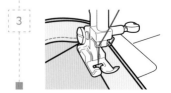 Working from the wrong side, edgestitch the bias tape in place.

HOW TO ATTACH DOUBLE-FOLD BIAS TAPE AS A BINDING

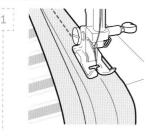

1

Double-fold bias tape has one fold narrower than the other. Lay the bias tape against the right side of the piece it will be sewn to with the narrow fold on top and to the right. Unfold the top fold twice so that the right edge of the bias tape and the item are aligned and pin in place. Stitch in the far-right crease. As for single-fold tape, line up the crease in the centre notch of the presser foot and use that as your seam guide.

2

Fold the bias tape over to the wrong side of the item to wrap the raw edges and press in place.

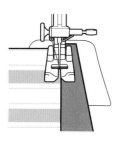

3

Working from the right side, stitch in the ditch. The fold is wider on the wrong side so you will be catching the fold even though you cannot see it. On the right side the stitches will be hidden in the seam and give a clean finish.

YOU WILL NEED:

- Double-fold bias tape (either ready-made or handmade)
- Pins
- Iron and ironing board

TIP

Single-fold bias tape is a great way to finish curved edges on armholes, necklines and hems since the bias allows the tape to bend smoothly. Double-fold bias tape can be used to bind edges on blankets, bibs, handbags and garments.

SEE ALSO

page 34: Bias tape
page 162: Hems
page 168: Facings
page 169: Linings

Piping and welting

YOU WILL NEED:

- Fabric to make continuous bias strips
- Cord
- Pins
- Zipper foot

TIP

Make sure the seam allowance is the same as the project you are working on to eliminate confusion.

HOW TO MAKE PIPING AND WELTING

1 Figure out how wide the bias strip will be. It should be twice the seam allowance plus the circumference of your cord. I am using 6mm (¼in) cord and 1.6cm (⅝in) seam allowances so my tape is 4.8cm (1⅞in) wide. Cut and make continuous bias strips the same way you would make them for bias tape.

2 With the bias strip wrong side up, lay the cord in the middle.

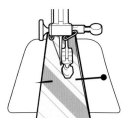

3 Fold the bias strip in half with wrong sides facing to encase the cord. Pin to hold in place.

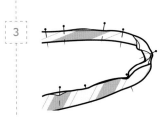

4 Put the zipper foot on your sewing machine. Line up the right edge of the cording against the left edge of the zipper foot and lower the presser foot. Stitch along the edge of the cording. You have piping!

SEE ALSO
page 21: Zipper feet
page 38: Piping, welting, and corded edges
page 128: How to make a continuous bias strip

SEWING ON PIPING AND WELTING

1 Lay your piping against the right side of the fabric piece it will be sewn to. Make sure that the raw edges of the piping and the item are aligned and pin in place.

2 Put the zipper foot on your sewing machine. Line up the right edge of the cording against the left edge of the zipper foot and lower the presser foot. Stitch along the edge of the cording.

3 Now place the lining or facing piece of fabric face down on top of the piping and pin in place.

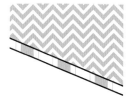

4 Again, line up the right edge of the cording against the left edge of the zipper foot and lower the presser foot. Move your needle to the left position to nestle it tightly against the cording. Stitch along the edge of the cording.

5 Turn right side and press.

YOU WILL NEED:

- Piping or welting (either ready-made or handmade)
- Pins
- Zipper foot
- Iron and ironing board

TIP

A piping foot has a groove on the bottom to accommodate the round shape of piping. It keeps the piping in place to allow perfectly even stitching without risk of stitching into the piping. Each size foot is designed for one size of piping, so you may need to buy several sizes. A standard zipper foot works well for all sizes of piping and welting.

SEE ALSO
page 21: Zipper feet
page 38: Piping, welting, and corded edges

Sewing on trims

YOU WILL NEED:

· Fabric marker or
  tailor's chalk
· Clear ruler, tape measure
  or seam gauge
· Satin-stitch foot
· Pins

TIP

I like to use a satin-stitch foot
because the clear plastic allows
for better visibility and the
groove on the bottom allows
space for trims. You can also
use an all-purpose/zigzag foot.

FLAT TRIMS

Flat trims such as ribbon, rickrack, lace and sequin trim can all be machine
topstitched on to fabric with a straight, zigzag or decorative stitch.

HOW TO ATTACH FLAT TRIMS DOWN THE MIDDLE

1 Mark placement for your trim on to the item on which it will be
stitched using a ruler and chalk or marker. Pin the trim in place.

2 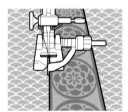 Align the trim in the middle of
the foot, lower the presser foot
and stitch down the middle
using the stitch of your choice.
You can use the centre groove
or notch on the foot as your
seam guide.

YOU WILL NEED:

· Fabric marker or
  tailor's chalk
· Clear ruler, tape measure
  or seam gauge
· Blind hem foot
· Pins

TIP

You can also edgestitch ribbons
using an all-purpose/zigzag
foot or a satin-stitch foot.

HOW TO ATTACH FLAT TRIMS ALONG THE EDGES

1 Mark placement for your trim on to the fabric on which it will
be stitched using a ruler and chalk or marker. Pin it in place.

2 Put the blind hem foot on your
machine. Using the hand screw,
adjust the bar on the foot so
that it comes right up against
the left edge of the trim. With
your needle in the centre
position, stitch down the left
edge of the trim.

3 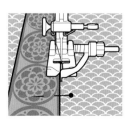 Now, adjust the bar on the
blind hem foot until it comes
to the right edge of the trim.
Stitch down the right edge of
the trim.

SEE ALSO
page 20: Hem feet
page 21: Embroidery
and quilting feet

HOW TO ATTACH FLAT TRIMS USING A TWIN NEEDLE

This works well for narrow trims that are 1cm (³⁄₈in) or smaller.

1 Mark placement for your trim on to the item on which it will be stitched using a ruler and chalk. Pin the trim in place.

2

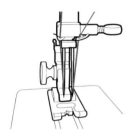

Insert the twin needle into the machine and then thread two threads through the machine. Rather than buying a second spool of thread, just wind a second bobbin and use this as your second thread. Make sure that the threads don't tangle as you thread them. Set the machine to a regular straight stitch. Because there is only one bobbin, the bobbin thread will zigzag back and forth between the two needle threads.

3

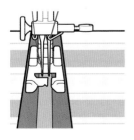

Line up the fabric so that the twin needle will stitch two rows of stitching down the middle of the trim.

YOU WILL NEED:

- Fabric marker or tailor's chalk
- Clear ruler, tape measure or seam gauge
- All-purpose/zigzag foot or a satin-stitch foot
- Twin needle that is slightly narrower than your trim

TIP

Any machine that can do a zigzag can use a twin needle, but make sure that the needles will fit through the hole in your presser foot.

SEE ALSO
page 25: Twin needles

Raised trims

YOU WILL NEED:

- Fabric marker or tailor's chalk
- Clear ruler, tape measure or seam gauge
- Zipper foot
- Pins

TIP

Try using a glue stick or basting tape instead of pins to hold your trims in place.

SEE ALSO
page 19: Zipper feet

You can handstitch or glue raised trims such as pearls, braided or beaded trims on to fabric. But it is much faster to machine stitch them down.

HOW TO ATTACH RAISED TRIMS ON THE EDGES

1 Mark placement for your trim on to the item on which it will be stitched using a ruler and chalk or marker. Pin the trim in place.

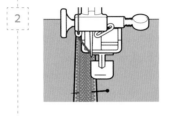

2 Put the zipper foot on your machine. Line up the right edge of the raised part of the trim against the left edge of the zipper foot and lower the presser foot. Stitch along the edge of the trim.

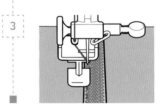

3 Move your zipper foot so that the left edge of the raised part of the trim is against the right edge of the zipper foot and lower the presser foot. Stitch along the edge of the trim.

YOU WILL NEED:

- Fabric marker or tailor's chalk
- Clear ruler, tape measure or seam gauge
- Satin-stitch foot
- Pins

HOW TO ATTACH RAISED TRIMS WITH A ZIGZAG

1 Mark placement for your trim on to the item on which it will be stitched using a ruler and chalk or marker. Pin the trim in place.

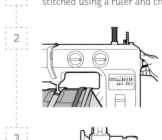

2 Set your machine to the widest zigzag. Align the trim in the middle of the foot, lower the presser foot and hand walk the needle to make sure the needle clears the raised part of the trim.

3 Zigzag down the middle. It is very helpful to use the centre groove or notch on the foot as your seam guide.

EDGE TRIMS

Edge trims such as fringe, ruffle, pom-pom and lace edgings are designed to have one side free while the either side is in a seam.

HOW TO ATTACH TRIMS ON AN EDGE

1

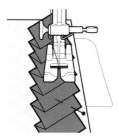

Draw in the seam allowance in the fabric on the right side. Lay your trim face down against the right side of the fabric piece it will be sewn to. Make sure that the edge of the trim is aligned on the line you drew and pin in place. Stitch on the edge of the trim.

2

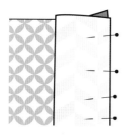

If the project has a lining or facing, place it face down on top of the piping and pin in place and stitch.

3

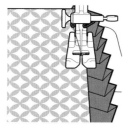

Turn right side and press. Topstitch or edgestitch if desired.

YOU WILL NEED:

- All-purpose foot
- Fabric marker
- Pins

TIP

For truly round trims such as pearls, try a piping foot. The round groove will hold the trim in place and allow you to zigzag over the beads. But you will need to handstitch delicate trims such as stones or crystals.

TIP

Rickrack can be sewn on an edge for a scalloped trim.

SEE ALSO

page 39: Pom pom, fringes and ruffles

Fabric appliqué

YOU WILL NEED:

- Lightweight fusible interfacing
- Iron and ironing board
- Pins
- Fabric marker
- Scissors

TIP

You can make your own iron-on appliqués by using a double-sided fusible instead of fusible interfacing. Follow all the same steps but after you cut out the shape, peel off the paper backing and it is ready to fuse on to your project.

You can purchase ready-made appliqués in many shapes and sizes. You can use a motif from a printed fabric or design your own shape from any fabric you like.

HOW TO MAKE AN APPLIQUÉ PATCH

1 Cut out a piece of fabric that is a little bit larger than your appliqué will be. My appliqué will be about 15cm (6in) square so I cut a 18cm (7in) square.

2 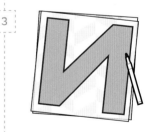 Cut out the same size of fusible interfacing. Apply the fusible to the wrong side of your fabric following the manufacturer's recommendations for iron temperature.

3 Using your fabric marker, draw your shape or trace off the shape from the print. Note that since you are drawing on the back, your image will be reversed. This is especially important when doing letters.

4 Cut out your shape on the line. Your appliqué is now ready to stitch on to your project!

SEE ALSO
page 32: Appliqué
page 86: Interfacing

HOW TO ATTACH AN APPLIQUÉ PATCH

1   Pin your appliqué face up on to the fabric it will be stitched to.

2   Set your machine to a wide zigzag stitch that is between 3 and 5mm and a short length of about 1mm. Install the satin stitch or appliqué stitch on your machine.

3    Turn the handwheel until the needle is on the right side of the zigzag and position your fabric so that the needle comes down just outside the edge of the appliqué.

4    Satin stitch all the way around your appliqué, leaving long thread tails at the beginning and end instead of backstitching.

5   Using a handsewing needle, pull the top thread tails through to the wrong side of the fabric and hand tie off.

YOU WILL NEED:

- Pins
- Satin-stitch foot or appliqué foot
- Handsewing needle

TIP

You could backstitch but it tends to look cleaner when you hand tie the tails. If you do backstitch, set your machine to a straight stitch to camouflage the backstitching. It looks very messy when you backstitch with a zigzag stitch.

SEE ALSO
page 21: *Embroidery and quilting feet*
page 32: *Appliqué*

CHAPTER 9
FITTING SOLUTIONS

No pattern in the world fits perfectly straight out of the envelope. Everyone has a unique figure and patterns come in a limited range of standardised sizes. Therefore, all patterns need to be altered to achieve perfect fit. In this chapter, we'll go over common fitting problems and how to fix them.

All about fit

What is good fit? It's actually pretty simple. The length grain of fabric should hang straight to the floor and hems should be parallel to the floor. Fabric should lay smoothly over the contours of the body without bunching, twisting or pulling. Muffin tops, squashed breasts and straining buttons are all signs that a garment is too small or that there's not enough fabric in a certain area. Sagging fabric, and gaping armholes, necklines and waists are all signs that there's too much fabric in a specific area. It can take a bit of time to get a pattern fitted correctly, but it is worth it! Once you have a well-fitting pattern then you can cut and sew it in tons of different fabrics. You can change necklines and skirt and sleeve lengths to create completely new looks.

There are two common ways to correct the fit of a pattern. One way is to cut a muslin. This means that you will cut and sew a practice garment in a low-quality fabric to check the fit. You can mark any fit issues right on the fabric with a marker or pencil. You can cut the fabric where it's too tight to allow it to relax and you can pin out excess fabric. You will want to mark along the pin lines where you have pinched out any excess fabric so that you can remove the pins and see your changes. If you have slashed to add in more fabric, measure how much the muslin spreads apart. You then transfer any changes to your pattern. Tissue fitting is another method, where you cut and pin the tissue paper pattern together along the seam lines and try it on. Just like with muslin, you can mark fit corrections, but in this case, it's right on the pattern.

Fitting a muslin

TIP

It is very difficult to fit yourself because, as you are twisting in front of a mirror to see from different angles, you are distorting the garment. If you do not have a sewing friend to help, I highly recommend working on a dress form.

You can also make a bodice and skirt sloper. A sloper is a fitting tool and is a basic pattern that is fitted to your body and will reflect all the unique curves and bumps and angles. Every major pattern company sells a sloper pattern. Once you have made and fitted a sloper, you can use it to adjust other patterns. Simply slide the corrected sloper pattern under a commercial tissue pattern and you will instantly see where you need to make adjustments.

SEE ALSO

page 70: Dress forms
page 82: Muslin
page 144: Making a muslin
page 145: Tissue fitting

Q. WHAT IS EASE?

A. Ease is the amount of space between the body and a garment. Every garment has ease in it but there is a difference between fitting ease and design ease.

Fitting ease is the extra room that allows you to move, sit and breathe. Even a corset has a bit of ease or you would not be able to expand your lungs! Stretch knits, however, can have negative ease where the garment is smaller than the body and will stretch to fit (for example, a swimsuit).

Design ease is about the look. A buttonfront shirt can be formfitting with little design ease or can be very boxy with lots of design ease. Both will have fitting ease but the extra design ease is up to the designer's vision. Most patterns will give you both finished garment measurements and body measurements and you can compare them to see how much ease is in the pattern.

Making a muslin

YOU WILL NEED:

- Cotton muslin fabric
- Contrasting all-purpose sewing thread
- Scissors
- Pins
- Marker or pencil

TIP

Muslins do not necessarily need to be made from cotton muslin. While muslin is the traditional fabric for test garments, you can use any low-quality fabric with a similar weight and drape to your actual fabric. If I am making a dress out of silk charmeuse, then polyester charmeuse makes a good muslin. If your garment is to be made out of a stretch fabric, then make sure your muslin is also made from a fabric with a similar amount of stretch.

When you make a test garment, you won't bother to cut and stitch details such as facings, linings, collars, pockets or closures and will only need to cut and stitch one sleeve.

1 Cut out all the main pattern pieces from the muslin. Mark your seam lines and grainlines on the muslin with the marker.

2

Baste together all darts and seam lines.

3

Try on the garment and pin the opening shut. Make a note of any problem areas.

4

Pin out excess fabric. Slash where it's too tight and note how much the muslin spreads.

SEE ALSO
page 82: Muslin
page 118: Darts, gathers and pleats

Tissue fitting

I like tissue fitting because it is faster than cutting a muslin. However, patterns give you only a half pattern so you won't be able to evaluate the whole garment. Note that tissue will never hang the same way as fabric and that this method does not work for garments with negative ease.

1 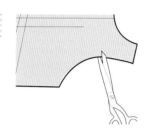 Cut out all the main pattern pieces from the pattern. Clip into seam allowances to allow them to spread along curves.

2 Pin together all darts and seam lines. Pin the front to the back along the seam lines at the shoulder and side seams. You should end up with a pattern for half a garment.

3  Put on the T-shirt or leggings. Carefully try on the pattern and pin the center front to your T-shirt or leggings centre front to anchor it. Do the same for the centre back. Make a note of any problem areas.

4 Pin out excess tissue. Slash where it's too tight and note how much the tissue spreads.

YOU WILL NEED:
- Scissors
- Pins
- Marker or pencil
- A snug-fitting T-shirt (for tops and dresses) or leggings (for skirts and trousers)

TIP
Iron fusible interfacing to the wrong side of tissue patterns to stabilise them. It makes them heavier so they do not float away with the slightest breeze and makes them stronger. Use a hot and DRY iron. Water and paper are a bad combination.

SEE ALSO
page 82: Muslin
page 111: Clipping and notching
page 118: Darts, gathers and pleats

Bust adjustments

YOU WILL NEED:

- Pencil and eraser
- Compass
- Clear ruler
- Pins or thread

TIP

All patterns are designed for a B cup. If you are bigger or smaller than a B cup, the bodice is never going to fit correctly through the bust. Some women have a high bust while others have a low bust. Some women have breasts that are close together while others have breasts that are further apart.

LOW OR HIGH BUST ADJUSTMENT

The apex is the fullest part of the bust and is frequently marked on a pattern with a circled plus sign. But the apex on the pattern may not be where your apex is. If darts end too close to the apex you will have a pointy bust. If they end too far away then you will have a poufy bust. Darts should end 1.3 to 2.5cm (½in to 1in) away from your apex. If your darts are too long or too short, this is a very easy fix.

When you are trying on your muslin or tissue pattern, mark your apex in the correct spot.

Take off the muslin or pattern, remove basting or pins and spread flat. With a compass, draw a circle around the apex. If you are a B cup or smaller make the circle 2.5cm (1in) diameter. If you are a larger cup then make the circle bigger – 1.3cm (½in) bigger per cup size.

Draw a line from the apex through the middle of the dart.

Redraw the dart legs so that they go from the line you just drew starting at the circle and ending at the wide ends of the dart. Pin or baste this new dart and try on the muslin or tissue pattern to check for fit.

SEE ALSO

page 54: *Rulers*
page 118: *Darts, gathers and pleats*

NARROW OR WIDE BUST ADJUSTMENT

The darts should point to the apex for a smooth look. If they do not, then the fabric tends to twist or you will have drag lines. Just like changing the length of a dart, this is very simple.

1 When you are trying on your muslin or tissue pattern, mark your apex in the correct spot.

2 Take off the muslin or pattern, remove basting or pins and spread flat. Draw a box around the dart.

3 Cut out the box, move it to the correct position and tape in place. Fill in the gap with pattern paper and tape.

4 Redraw seam lines. Pin or baste this new dart and try on the muslin or tissue pattern to check for fit.

YOU WILL NEED:

- Pattern paper
- Scissors
- Pencil and eraser
- Clear ruler
- Adhesive tape

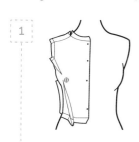

SEE ALSO
page 54: Rulers
page 68: Pattern paper
page 118: Darts, gathers and pleats

YOU WILL NEED:

- Pattern paper
- Scissors
- Pencil and eraser
- Adhesive tape
- Clear ruler
- Pins or thread

FULL BUST ADJUSTMENT

1

When you are trying on your muslin or tissue pattern, slash at the bust to allow the material to spread. Note how far it spreads. Take off the muslin or pattern, remove basting or pins and spread flat.

2

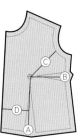

Working with the pattern, draw a line from the apex to the waist through the dart. Make sure the line is parallel to the centre front (line A). Draw a line from the apex through the middle of the side bust dart (B). Draw a line from the apex to the middle of the armhole (C). Draw a horizontal line from line A to the centre front 10cm (4in) from the bottom (D).

3

Cut along line A. Cut along line B. Cut line C, but stop just short of the armhole seam. Snip into the seam allowance and stop just short of the seam. You want to have a little hinge of paper there.

4

Spread the pattern apart at line A the amount you noted in step 1. Both darts will get bigger. Cut along line D and lower the piece until it is level with the waist.

5

Pin or baste the new darts and try on the muslin or tissue pattern to check for fit.

SEE ALSO

page 54: Rulers
page 66: Pattern paper
page 118: Darts, gathers and pleats

SMALL BUST ADJUSTMENT

YOU WILL NEED:

- Pencil and eraser
- Marker
- Adhesive tape
- Clear ruler
- Pins or thread

1

When trying on your muslin or tissue pattern, pinch out a vertical tuck until the bust is smooth. Write down the size of the total tuck. Take off the muslin or pattern, remove basting or pins and spread flat.

2

Working with the pattern, draw a line from the apex to the waist through the dart. Make sure the line is parallel to the centre front (line A). Draw a line from the apex through the middle of the side bust dart (B). Draw a line from the apex to the middle of the armhole (C). Draw a horizontal line from line A to the centre front 10cm (4in) from the bottom (D).

3

Cut along line A. Cut along line B. Cut line C, but stop just short of the armhole seam. Snip into the seam allowance and stop just short of the seam so you have a little hinge of paper there.

4

Overlap the pattern at line A by the amount you noted in step 1. Both darts will get smaller. Cut along line D and raise the piece until it is level with the waist.

5

Pin or baste the new darts and try on the pattern to check for fit.

SEE ALSO
page 54: Rulers
page 68: Pattern paper
page 118: Darts, gathers and pleats

Hips and rise

YOU WILL NEED:

- Pins
- Marker
- Pattern paper
- Pencil and eraser
- Adhesive tape
- Clear ruler
- French curve or design ruler
- Pins or thread

It's very easy to change the width of the hips to make them narrower or wider or to change the curve.

NARROW OR WIDE HIPS

1 Pin or baste any waist darts and then pin or baste the front to the back at the side seams. Try on your muslin or tissue pattern. If it is too loose, you will see vertical wrinkles. If it is too tight you will see horizontal wrinkles.

2 For narrow hips, pin out the excess along the side seam. Mark the pin lines and transfer the corrected side seam to your pattern using your straight and curves rulers and a pencil.

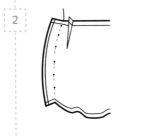

3 For wide hips, slash from the hem up to the waist to add width. Note how wide it spreads. Correct your pattern and fill in the gap with pattern paper. Redraw seam lines as needed.

SEE ALSO

page 54: Rulers
page 55: Speciality measuring tools
page 68: Pattern paper
page 118: Darts, gathers and pleats
page 144: Making a muslin

4 Pin or baste the new side seam and try on the muslin or tissue pattern to check for fit.

HIGH OR LOW HIPS

1

Try on your muslin or tissue pattern. Repin the side seam to reflect your hip curve, letting out where it is tight and taking in where it is loose. Make sure to keep the side seam straight to the floor. You do not want it angling forwards or backwards.

- Pins
- Marker
- Pencil and eraser
- Clear ruler
- French curve or design ruler
- Pins or thread

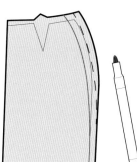

2

Mark the pin lines and transfer the corrected side seam to your pattern using your straight and curves rulers.

3

Pin or baste the new side seam and try on the muslin or tissue pattern to check for fit.

151

YOU WILL NEED:

- Tape measure or flexible ruler
- Marker
- Pattern paper
- Pencil and eraser
- Adhesive tape
- Clear ruler
- French curve or design ruler
- Thread

Q. WHAT IS THE RISE?

A. It is the crotch seam on trousers that goes from the centre front waist under and up to the centre back waist. This is the big problem area when fitting trousers; for example, you might have a flat or a round backside. These issues can all be fixed by altering the rise seam. For a perfect rise seam, take a well-fitting pair of pants and trace off the crotch curve on to your pants pattern.

CHANGING THE RISE

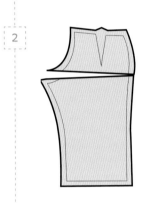

1

Baste together a muslin and try it on. Ask a friend to help because it is impossible to do this yourself. If it is tight over the buttocks, slash horizontally to release fabric and note how much it spreads. If it is loose, pin out a horizontal tuck and mark the pin line with your marker. Measure how much you pinched out.

2

To add fabric for a larger backside, slash your pattern from the centre back to the side seam above the crotch line but stop just short of the side seam. Snip into the seam allowance. You want to have a little hinge of paper there. Spread to lengthen the centre back seam to accommodate a larger backside. Fill in with pattern paper. Redraw the centre back seam using your curves and pencil. You can do the same thing on the front rise for a larger tummy.

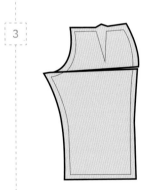

3

To remove fabric for a smaller backside, slash your pattern from the centre back to the side seam above the crotch line, but stop just short of the side seam. Snip into the seam allowance, so you have a little hinge of paper there. Overlap to shorten the centre back seam. Redraw the centre back seam with curves and pencil.

4

Baste a new muslin with the alterations and check for fit.

Waistline

The waist tends to have two main problems. It is either higher or lower than the pattern or it is wider or narrower.

LONG-WAISTED

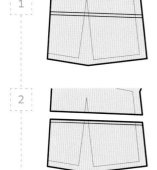

1 Your pattern should have a pair of parallel lines at the waist. This is where you can add length.

2 Cut the pattern apart on these lines and spread apart to the distance needed, keeping the pieces parallel. Fill in the gap with pattern paper and tape in place.

3 Repeat for the back piece so that the side seams still match up.

SHORT-WAISTED

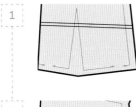

1 Your pattern should have a pair of parallel lines at the waist. This is where you can remove length.

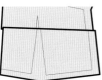

2 Cut the pattern apart on these lines and overlap the pieces by the amount needed, keeping them parallel and tape in place.

3 Repeat for the back piece so that the side seams still match up.

YOU WILL NEED:

- Pattern paper
- Adhesive tape
- Scissors
- Clear ruler
- Pencil and eraser

TIP

Elastic thread is a great way to take in fabric anywhere on a garment but it looks especially nice at the waist. Hand wind elastic thread on the bobbin and stitch parallel rows of straight stitching wherever you want to bring in a garment. You can do this all around a waist, just at the back waist, under the bust or at sleeve hems.

YOU WILL NEED:

- Clear ruler
- Adhesive tape
- Pencil and eraser

SEE ALSO

page 29: Elastic thread
page 54: Rulers
page 68: Pattern paper

YOU WILL NEED:

- Marker
- Clear ruler
- French curve or design ruler
- Pencil and eraser
- Pins or thread

TIP

You can also make the darts wider. This will bring in the waist. But do not make the darts too wide or they will create a pouf at the dart point.

MAKE THE WAIST SMALLER

1 To take in a waist, you can simply pin out the excess fabric at the side seams. Starting at the hips, pin out the excess material up to the waistline.

2 Mark the pin lines and transfer the corrected side seam to your pattern using your straight and curves rulers.

3 Pin or baste the new side seam and try on the muslin or tissue pattern to check for fit.

YOU WILL NEED:

- Pattern paper
- Adhesive tape
- Clear ruler
- Pencil and eraser
- Pins or sewing thread

| SEE ALSO |

page 54: Rulers
page 55: Speciality measuring tools
page 144: Making a muslin
page 145: Tissue fitting

MAKE THE WAIST LARGER

1 To let out a waist, you can remove darts. Remove the basting stitches on your muslin or pins on your tissue. Let the waist spread. If you need more room in the waist, let out the side seams at the waist. Repin up to the waist to fit.

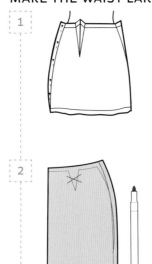

2 Repeat steps 2 and 3 as above to complete the alteration.

Shoulders and sleeves

Some people have square shoulders while others have sloping shoulders. Shoulders can be wide or narrow. Tops, jackets and dresses all hang from the shoulders so it is important that garments fit well here.

YOU WILL NEED:

- Pattern paper
- Pencil and eraser
- Adhesive tape
- Clear ruler
- Pins or thread

SQUARE OR SLOPING SHOULDERS

1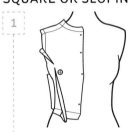

Try on your muslin or tissue pattern. Repin the shoulder seam to reflect your shoulder line, letting out where it is tight and taking in where it is loose. Keep the shoulder seam straight – you do not want it angling forwards or backwards.

2

Mark the pin lines and transfer the corrected shoulder seam to your pattern using your straight ruler. Tape in additional pattern paper as needed.

3

Raise or lower the top of the side seam by the same amount as the shoulder is raised or lowered at the armhole. This will ensure that the armhole length stays the same and the sleeve will still fit.

4

Pin or baste the new shoulder seam and try on the muslin or tissue pattern to check for fit.

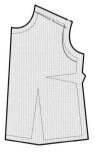

┆ SEE ALSO ┆

page 54: Rulers
page 55: Speciality measuring tools
page 144: Making a muslin
page 145: Tissue fitting

YOU WILL NEED:

- Pattern paper
- Pencil and eraser
- Adhesive tape
- Clear ruler

TIP

If you have uneven shoulders where one shoulder is higher than the other, try putting a small shoulder pad on the lower shoulder.

WIDE OR NARROW SHOULDERS

1 Try on your muslin or tissue pattern. The shoulder seam should end right at the shoulder joint. To find the joint, raise your arm and feel the little indentation where your arm joins your shoulder.

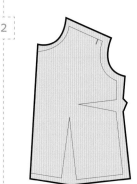

2 If your shoulders are narrow, mark where the shoulder should end on your muslin or tissue with a marker.

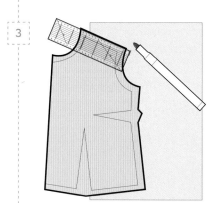

3 If your shoulders are wide, measure out where the shoulder should end with your ruler.

4 Transfer the corrected shoulder seam to your pattern using your straight ruler. Tape in additional pattern paper as needed.

 SEE ALSO

page 54: *Rulers*
page 55: *Speciality measuring tools*
page 144: *Making a muslin*
page 145: *Tissue fitting*

LARGE UPPER ARMS

1

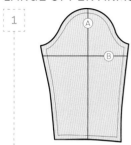

Measure your bicep and compare this measurement to the sleeve pattern bicep. There should be a minimum of 2.5cm (1in) of ease for a very fitted sleeve and 5 to 8cm (2 to 3in) for a looser fit. Draw a straight line on the pattern from the sleeve cap down to the wrist. This is line A. Draw a line across the bicep. This is line B.

2

Cut along line A and line B. Stop just short of the seams. Snip into the seam allowance and stop just short of the seam. You want to have a little hinge of paper there.

3

Spread the pattern apart at line A by the amount you noted in step 1. Let the cap lower and overlap on to the sleeve.

4

Fill in the gap with pattern paper and tape. Use your curved ruler to smooth out the curve on the top of the sleeve cap.

YOU WILL NEED:

- Pattern paper
- Pencil and eraser
- Adhesive tape
- Clear ruler
- French curve or design ruler

TIP

You can always change from long to short sleeves. Mark the finished length on the pattern and then add on the hem allowance.

Neckline

YOU WILL NEED:
- Pencil and eraser
- French curve or design ruler

TIPS

I always like to make sure that the neckline covers my bra straps.

If you change the neckline, remember to change the facing or lining to match.

You can change a neckline for fit or simply to change the look of a piece.

WIDEN OR NARROW A NECKLINE

1   Mark the new neckline width on the shoulder line on your pattern.

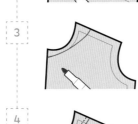

2   Using your curved ruler, blend from the new width to the centre front.

3   Repeat for the back neckline, making sure that the shoulder seams match.

4   Add a seam allowance to the new neckline.

YOU WILL NEED:
- Pencil and eraser
- French curve or design ruler

SEE ALSO
page 54: Rulers
page 55: Speciality measuring tools

RAISE OR LOWER A NECKLINE

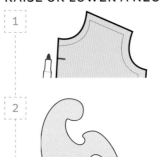

1   Mark the new neckline drop on the centre front on your pattern.

2   Using your curved ruler, blend from the new centre front to the shoulder.

3 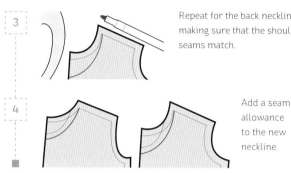 Repeat for the back neckline, making sure that the shoulder seams match.

TIP

Be careful with wide and deep V necks or you risk the garment sliding off your shoulders.

4 Add a seam allowance to the new neckline.

CHANGE THE NECKLINE SHAPE

You can redraw any neckline shape to a different shape, such as a scoop neck, V neck, sweetheart neckline, square or bateau.

1 Mark the new neckline drop on the centre front of the pattern. Mark the new neckline width on the shoulder seam of the pattern.

2 Using your curved ruler, blend from the new centre front to the shoulder.

3 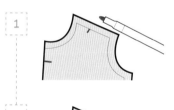 Repeat for the back neckline, making sure that the shoulder seams match.

4  Add a seam allowance to the new neckline.

YOU WILL NEED:

- Pencil and eraser
- Clear ruler
- French curve or design ruler

Q. WHY ARE FRONT AND BACK NECKLINES DIFFERENT LENGTHS?

A. It helps the garment to hang correctly from the shoulders. If the front and backlines have the same depths, the garment will always shift forwards. So the back neckline is almost always higher than the front.

SEE ALSO
page 54: Rulers
page 55: Speciality measuring tools

CHAPTER 10
FINISHING
SOLUTIONS

Finishing techniques such as hems, facings and closures can really make or break a project. When they are done well, your project looks professional, so do not rush through these final steps. Once you master these basic and simple techniques, you will find you use them over and over.

Hems

YOU WILL NEED:

- Sewing gauge
- Iron and ironing board
- Glass-head pins

TIP

If you would like the stitch line closer to the fold, try lining up the fold in the centre groove of your presser foot and adjust the needle to the right position and topstitch. Note that not all machines have a needle right position.

Patterns often tell you to hem a garment and offer just one option. There are lots of different ways to finish hems on skirts, trousers, dresses, tops and sleeves, and you can use whichever type you prefer.

DOUBLE TURN-BACK AND TOPSTITCHED

This is the most common hem you see. It simply involves turning the raw edge under twice and then stitching it.

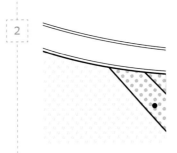

1 Press the hem to the wrong side the full amount of your hem allowance. I find it super-helpful to use a seam gauge and to pin the fabric to the ironing board. Make sure to use glass-head pins (not plastic) so you can press right over the pins.

2 Unfold and turn the edge under by 6mm (¼in) and press again. Re-fold and pin the hem for sewing.

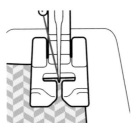

3 Working from the wrong side, line up the fold against the left edge of the presser foot and adjust your needle to the left position. Topstitch in place.

SEE ALSO
page 54: Basic measuring tools
page 60: Pins

SINGLE TURN-BACK AND TOPSTITCHED

This hem does not look quite as finished as the double turn-back but is really common on ready-to-wear clothing because it is fast and easy.

 1   Finish the raw edge of your hem by serging.

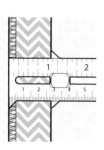

2   Press the hem to the wrong side the full amount of your hem allowance. Use the seam gauge to make sure it is accurate.

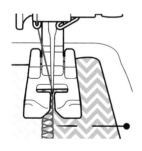

3   Now, switch back to a sewing machine. Pin the hem and line up the right edge of the serge stitch under the centre of your presser foot and topstitch.

YOU WILL NEED:

- Serger
- Iron and ironing board
- Sewing gauge
- Pins

TIP

If you don't have a serger, you can use an overcast foot and a zigzag or overcast stitch.

SEE ALSO

page 20: Seam finishing feet
page 116: Seam finishes

YOU WILL NEED:

- Iron and ironing board
- Twin needle
- Sewing gauge
- Pins

TIP

Rather than buying a second spool of thread, just wind a second bobbin and use that as your second thread.

FAUX COVERSTITCH USING A TWIN NEEDLE

A real coverstitch is done on a coverstitch machine, but most of us do not have this gadget. Not to worry! You can do a faux coverstitch on a regular sewing machine using a twin needle and a basic straight stitch. Because there is only one bobbin, the bobbin thread will zigzag back and forth between the two needle threads, and the seam can stretch.

1 Finish the raw edge and then press the hem under to the wrong side.

2 Insert the twin needle into the sewing machine.

3

Thread the machine with two threads, making sure that the threads do not tangle as you thread them.

4

Working from the right side, line up the fabric so that the twin needle will stitch right on the edge.

SEE ALSO

page 16: The serger/ overlock machine

page 24: Machine needles

BLIND HEM

This hem adds a classy touch to trousers, skirts and dresses where you do not want to see stitches on the right side. A blind hem is not as strong as a topstitched hem, so you should reserve it for garments that will be dry-cleaned or handwashed.

YOU WILL NEED:

- Iron and ironing board
- Sewing gauge
- Pins
- Blind hem foot

TIP

If you see a big stitch on the right side, then you stitched too much on to the fold. The blind hem can be tricky, so take your time and practice!

1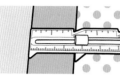
Press up your hem to the wrong side the full amount.

2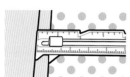
Now fold your hem back to the wrong side so that 6mm (¼in) of the raw edge extends out.

3 Adjust your machine to the blind hem stitch (on my machine it is stitch E). The little zigzags will finish the raw edge.

4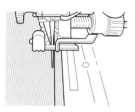
Put the blind hem foot on your machine. Using the handwheel, walk your machine until the needle swings to far-left zigzag. You want the needle to just barely catch the fold.

5 Using the handscrew, adjust the bar on the foot so that it comes right up against the fold. This will keep the stitch nice and even.

6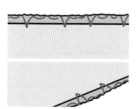
The big zigzag will catch just a thread of the fold and the little zigzags will finish the raw edge and prevent fraying.

7
Unfold the hem and press it flat. From the right side you should barely be able to see a tiny stitch every 1.3cm (½in) or so.

SEE ALSO
page 20: Hem feet

YOU WILL NEED:

- Rolled hem foot
- Iron and ironing board
- Pin or seam ripper

TIP

Spray the edge of your fabric with laundry spray starch and iron the fabric dry. This will make the fabric stiffer and easier to control.

ROLLED HEM: SEWING MACHINE

A rolled hem is a very pretty finish on sheer fabrics such as chiffon and looks wonderful on dresses, blouses and scarves.

1 Press your hem to the wrong side 3mm (⅛in) and then press under another 3mm.

2  Install the rolled hem on your sewing machine.

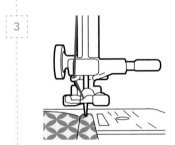

3 Take a couple of stitches on the hem edge, and with the needle in the fabric, lift the presser foot.

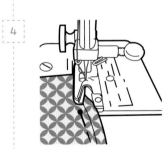

4 Use a seam ripper or pin to gently guide the hem into the scroll of the rolled hem foot and then lower the presser foot.

5 Stitch the hem.

SEE ALSO
page 20: Hem feet

ROLLED HEM: SERGER

Rolled hems can be done on a standard machine but this is MUCH faster and easier! This is a fantastic way to quickly hem napkins and ruffles.

1   Thread your serger for three-thread serging. There is no need for the second needle thread.

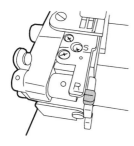

2   Disengage the stitch finger. On most sergers, you simply pull a switch to slide the finger forwards and out of the way. For other sergers, the stitch finger is attached to the needle plate and you switch to a rolled hem plate. Be sure to check your manual.

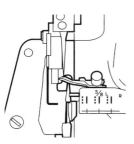

3   Disengage or remove the upper knife. Usually this is as easy as turning a knob.

4   Shorten your stitch length to 3.8mm (1½in).

5   With your fabric face up, slide it under the presser foot and start stitching. You will see how the fabric folds under as the threads stitch over the edge.

YOU WILL NEED:

- Serger

TIP

When working with knit fabrics, you can stretch the fabric to create a ruffled lettuce edge.

SEE ALSO
page 16: The serger/ overlock machine

Facings

YOU WILL NEED:

- Fusible interfacing
- Scissors
- Iron and ironing board
- Pins
- Handsewing needle

TIP

You can use single-fold bias tape as a facing on armholes, necklines and waists. The bias tape will curve around these edges. It is very quick since you do not have to cut out facing pieces from your fabric.

A facing is a piece of fabric on the inside of a garment, used to finish edges neatly. It is often used on curved edges where it would be hard to fold over the edge and stitch it. The facing ranges from 2.5 to 8cm (1in to 3in) wide and can be interfaced to provide support to the edge.

HOW TO SEW A FACING

1   Cut out your facing pieces from the fabric and the fusible interfacing. Cut off the seam allowances from the interfacing to eliminate bulk at the seams. Apply the interfacing to the wrong side of the facing, following the manufacturer's recommendations for iron temperature.

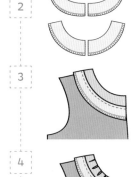

2   Finish the bottom edge of the facing by serging, pinking, overcasting or clean finish.

3   Place the facing right sides together with the main piece, lining up the raw edges, and pin in place. Stitch along the seam lines.

4   Clip the curves so the seam allowance will lay flat when they are turned right side out.

5   Press the seam allowances towards the facing. Understitch the facing to the seam allowance.

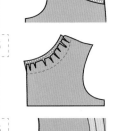

6   Turn right side out and press. Handtack the facing to the seam allowances at the shoulder seams or side seams to prevent the facing from flipping out to the right side.

SEE ALSO
page 130: How to attach single-fold bias tape as a facing

Linings

A lining is a separate thin layer on the inside of the garment. It is a duplicate of the outside and can be constructed in the same way. A lining can be used with a facing or on its own.

HOW TO LINE A SLEEVELESS BODICE

It is easy to line a bodice even if the pattern has no instructions or pattern pieces for a lining. It is perfect for slightly sheer fabrics where facings would show. The front or back bodice must have an opening.

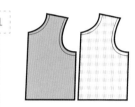

1 Cut the front and back bodice pieces from the main fabric and then cut them again from the lining fabric. Staystitch the neckline and armholes on both the outside and lining pieces to stop them from stretching.

2 Stitch the outside pieces together at the shoulder seams and press the seam allowances open. Do the same for the lining pieces.

3 Place the lining and outside together with right sides facing, and pin the neckline, armholes, and front/back opening. Stitch together at the neckline, armholes and front/back opening.

4 Clip the curves and corners. Turn right side out and press. Place outside right sides facing and linings right sides facing and pin and stitch the side seams.

YOU WILL NEED:

- Scissors
- Iron and ironing board
- Pins

Q. WHAT IS UNDERSTITCHING?

A. Understitching is used to keep garment linings and facings from rolling forwards to the outside. After you press the seam allowances towards the facing or lining, turn the garment so that the facing or lining is face up. Stitch again 3mm (⅛in) or less away from the seam, stitching through both the facing/lining and both seam allowances.

SEE ALSO

page 86: Interfacing
page 86: Linings
page 111: Clipping and notching

Buttonholes

YOU WILL NEED:

- Manual buttonhole foot
- Chalk or fabric marker

Sewing machines tend to do one of two types of buttonholes: either a four-step manual buttonhole or a one-step automatic buttonhole. Usually mechanical machines do the four-step and computerised machines do the automatic type.

FOUR-STEP MANUAL BUTTONHOLE

1 Place your buttonhole foot on the sewing machine.

2 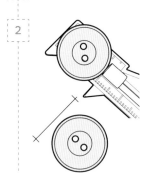 Mark your buttonhole on the fabric using chalk or fabric marker.

3 Adjust the pattern selector to buttonhole step 1 and the stitch length to 0.5mm. Adjust the slider so that your marking is perfectly framed in the window.

4  Zigzag down the left side of the buttonhole until you get to the bottom. You will notice the window sliding closed as you stitch down towards the bottom. Make sure that the last stitch is on the left side of the zigzag and that the needle is out of the fabric.

5 Adjust the selector to buttonhole step 2 and do five stitches (or any odd number so that you finish on the right side). The stitch will automatically adjust to a wider and shorter zigzag. Make sure the needle is out of the fabric when you finish the last stitch.

6

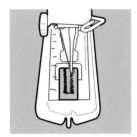

Adjust the selector to buttonhole step 3 and zigzag back up to the top. You will be going in reverse but you do not need to hold the backstitch button since this is part of the programmed stitch. As you sew, the window will slide back open. Make sure the last stitch is on the right and that the needle is out of the fabric.

Q: HOW BIG SHOULD YOU MAKE YOUR BUTTONHOLE?

A: The general rule of thumb is that the buttonhole should be the diameter of the button, plus the height of the button, plus 3mm (⅛in). You need to add in the height because ball or half-ball buttons need the buttonhole to open wider than flat buttons. The extra 3mm (⅛in) gives a little bit of wiggle room so that the buttonhole does not come out too small.

7

Adjust the selector to step 4 (often the same as step 2) and do five stitches. Make sure the needle is out of the fabric when you finish the last stitch.

8 Now you need to lock in the stitch, so adjust the selector to straight stitch and change your stitch length to 0mm and do three to four stitches.

9 Your buttonhole is done. Trim off your thread tails and admire your work!

SEE ALSO
page 19: *Buttonhole and button feet*
page 42: *Buttons*

YOU WILL NEED:

- Automatic buttonhole foot
- Chalk or fabric marker

TIP

Always do a couple of practice buttonholes on a scrap of the fabric you will be using. Some fabrics, such as knits or flannel, do not feed very easily and you may need a longer stitch length. Once you have done a practice one, cut it open and make sure that your button goes through easily.

ONE-STEP BUTTONHOLE

When you are making a one-step buttonhole, note that some machines start at the top and work their way around anti-clockwise. Other machines (like the one I am using) start at the bottom and work their way around clockwise. Always do a practice buttonhole to be sure.

1 Insert your button into the slot on the back of the buttonhole foot. This will slide the window to the correct size to fit that particular button. Since this will not take into account the height of the button, if you are using a ball button then you should use a keyhole buttonhole. Flat buttons can use either a box or rounded buttonhole. Install the foot on your machine.

2 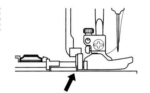 Lower the buttonhole lever so that it is between the two tabs.

3 Adjust your pattern selector to buttonhole stitch.

4 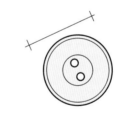 Mark your buttonholes on the fabric with chalk or a fabric marker.

5 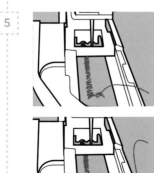 Position the foot so that you are starting at the beginning. Press the foot pedal and start stitching. The machine will stitch one side, across the top, back down and then across the bottom all in one step. When the buttonhole is done, the machine will do a couple of lock stitches to secure and may even beep at you to tell you it is done.

SEE ALSO

page 19: *Buttonhole and button feet*
page 42: *Buttons*

CUTTING OPEN A BUTTONHOLE: OPTION 1

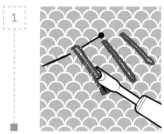

Place a pin through the top bartack and then, starting from the bottom bartack, carefully slide the seam ripper up through the centre of the buttonhole. The pin will form a stopper and will prevent you from slicing too far.

YOU WILL NEED:

· Seam ripper and a pin

CUTTING OPEN A BUTTONHOLE: OPTION 2

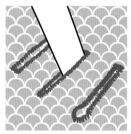

Place the wood under your buttonhole and use the chisel to slice open the buttonhole.

For keyhole buttonholes, use the hole cutter to cut open the round end.

YOU WILL NEED:

· Buttonhole cutting kit (contains a chisel, hole cutter, and wood block)

TIP

Apply seam sealant to your buttonhole after you cut it open to prevent the threads from fraying.

SEE ALSO

page 61: Seam rippers
page 65: Seam sealant

Buttons

YOU WILL NEED:

· Button foot
· Handsewing needle

SEWING ON A BUTTON BY MACHINE

While shank buttons must be sewn on by hand, you can stitch on sew-through buttons by machine. You will be amazed at how quick and easy this is!

1 Install the button foot on your machine.

2 Adjust your stitch selector to the widest zigzag and adjust the stitch length to 0mm.

3  Align your button in position and then lower the presser foot down so that the holes are between the toes.

4 Using the handwheel, manually walk the needle down into one hole and back up and down into the other hole. You may need to adjust the stitch width to make sure the needle goes in the holes. Once you are sure, let it zigzag back and forth about a dozen times. If you have a four-hole button, then just rotate the button to do the second set of holes.

5 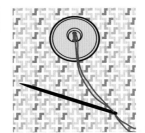 Make sure to leave long tails when you are done stitching. Then thread the top tails through a handsewing needle and pull them through to the back side. Knot them off and clip the threads.

SEE ALSO
page 19: *Buttonhole and button feet*
page 42: *Buttons*

Grommets and eyelets

Once you have set eyelets then you can thread ribbon or fabric through them.

1 Apply fusible interfacing to the wrong side of your fabric.

2 Mark placement for the eyelet with the marker and cut it open with an X-shaped slit.

3 Put the eyelet setting base on a hard surface and place the eyelet in the base.

4 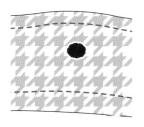 Lay your fabric over the eyelet face down and push the eyelet through the opening.

5  If it is a two-part eyelet or grommet, then place the top part of the eyelet over the stem. Insert the setter in the hole and hammer in place.

YOU WILL NEED:

- Fabric marker or tailor's chalk
- Fusible interfacing
- Scissors
- Eyelets
- Eyelet setter set and hammer

TIP

You can also get specially designed pliers to apply eyelets.

SEE ALSO

page 43: *Hardware*
page 86: *Interfacing*

Snaps

YOU WILL NEED:

- Thread
- Handsewing needle
- Needle threader
- Fabric marker or
  tailor's chalk
- Snap set

Sew-on snaps are best for areas where there is little strain. No-sew snaps are stronger and sturdier.

SEW-ON SNAPS

1 | Thread a handsewing needle with thread. You can use polyester, cotton, silk or topstitching thread.

2 |  Mark your snap placement with fabric marker or chalk.

3 |  Handstitch the ball half of the snap to the wrong side of the overlapping section by stitching through the holes around the edges. Be sure to only stitch through the facing layer so that the stitches do not show on the right side. You should do two to three stitches through each hole.

4 | Handstitch the socket half of the snap to the wrong side of the underlapping section in the same manner as the ball half, but you can stitch through all the layers of fabric.

 SEE ALSO

page 22: Handsewing
needles
page 28: Threads
page 45: Snaps

NO-SEW SNAPS

No-sew snaps have four parts. The cap and socket go together on the overlapping section and the stud and post go together on the underlapping section. Both the cap and the post have a stem that will flatten out into its mate to grip the fabric securely.

1. Mark your snap placement with fabric marker or chalk.

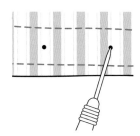

2. Punch holes for the snap stems using the awl.

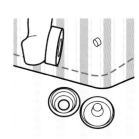

3. Load the pliers with the snap cap and socket. Align the stems through the punched holes and squeeze the pliers hard to apply.

4. Load the pliers with the stud and post using the adapter provided. Align the stems through the punched holes and squeeze the pliers hard to apply.

SEE ALSO
page 45: Snaps
page 69: Pattern notchers and awls

YOU WILL NEED:

- Snap pliers
- Fabric marker or tailor's chalk
- Awl
- Snap set

TIP

Once no-sew snaps are applied, they are nearly impossible to remove. Before you start, try a couple of practice ones on a scrap of fabric. If you do not have snap pliers, you can use a specially designed setter (often sold as a kit with the snaps) and a household hammer.

Hook-and-loop tape

YOU WILL NEED:
- Zipper foot
- Pins

TIP
Make sure that the hook side is away from the body to avoid scratching the skin.

Hook-and-loop tape comes in sew-on, self-adhesive and fusible varieties. The sew-on is the most secure type.

1 Install the zipper foot on your sewing machine.

2

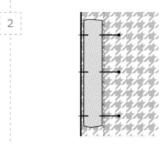

Place the hook side of the tape on the underlapping section and pin in place.

3

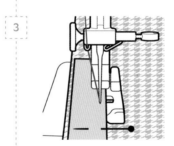

Edgestitch around the edges of the tape, making sure to backstitch at the beginning and end.

4

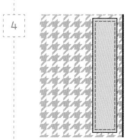

Place the loop side of the tape on the overlapping section and pin in place. Edgestitch it in place.

SEE ALSO

page 19: Zipper feet
page 46: Hook-and-loop fasteners

Buckles

Buckles are perfect for making your own custom belts and for making adjustable purse straps.

1 Measure the inside of your buckle to determine how wide your strap should be. My buckle measures 2.5mm (1in) wide. Cut a piece of fabric that is twice that width plus 2.5mm (1in) for the seam allowance and then the length of the strap. To make a belt, my piece measures 8cm (3in) wide and 94cm (37in) long.

2 Apply fusible interfacing to the wrong side of the fabric.

3  Fold the short ends in 1.3cm (½in) towards the wrong side and then fold in half with right sides facing and pin in place. Stitch the long side with a 1.3cm (½in) seam allowance and turn right side out. Press.

4 Edgestitch the short ends.

5 Mark placement for the buckle prong and cut it open with the awl.

6 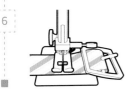 Thread the strap through the buckle and align the prong through the hole. Topstitch the folded back piece in place to secure.

YOU WILL NEED:

· Fabric marker
· Ruler
· Scissors
· Fusible interfacing
· Loop turner
· Iron and ironing board
· Awl

TIP

You can then apply eyelets to the other end of the strap to complete your belt.

SEE ALSO

page 43: Hardware
page 63: Loop turners
page 69: Pattern notchers and awls

D-rings and O-rings

YOU WILL NEED:

- Fabric marker
- Ruler
- Scissors
- Loop turner
- Iron and ironing board

TIP

You can thread a much wider strap through a ring for a soft, gathered look.

D-rings and O-rings can add an edge to handbags and accessories. Use them to make a three-part handle where one main section connects to ends that are threaded through rings.

1 Measure the inside of your ring to determine how wide your strap should be. My ring is 3.8cm (1½in) wide. Cut a piece of fabric that is twice that width plus 2.5cm (1in) for the seam allowance and twice the length plus 2.5cm (1in) seam allowance. My piece is 10cm (4in) wide and 20cm (8in) long.

2 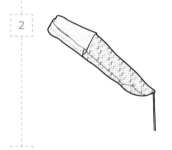 Fold in half with right sides facing and pin in place. Stitch the long side with a 1.3cm (½in) seam allowance and turn right side out.

3 Press flat.

4 Thread the strap through the ring and edgestitch the short ends together.

5 Stitch the strap to your main fabric with right sides together.

SEE ALSO

page 43: Hardware
page 63: Loop turners

Hooks and eyes

Hooks and eye closures can be used to anchor the top of a zip opening on skirts and dresses.

1 Thread a handsewing needle. You can use polyester, cotton, silk or topstitching thread.

2 Mark your hook and eye placement with fabric marker or tailor's chalk.

3 Handstitch the hook half to the wrong side of the overlapping section by stitching through the holes around the edges. Be sure to stitch only through the facing layer so that the stitches do not show on the right side. You should do two to three stitches through each hole.

4 Handstitch the eye half of the snap to the wrong side of the underlapping section in the same manner as the ball half, but you can stitch through all the layers of fabric.

YOU WILL NEED:
- Thread
- Handsewing needle
- Needle threader
- Fabric marker or tailor's chalk
- Hook and eye set

TIP
If you have matching edges rather than overlapping edges, then you will use the round eye instead of the bar eye.

SEE ALSO ⟩
page 22: Handsewing needles
page 28: Threads
page 44: Hooks and eyes

Zips

YOU WILL NEED:

· All-purpose foot

TIP

This method works only with standard coil zips, not for invisible zips. If you need a perfect colour match for an invisible zip, simply paint the pull with craft paint or nail polish.

Sometimes you cannot find the right length of zip in the colour you need. Don't worry – you can always shorten a zip! But you cannot make a zip longer, so always go longer rather than shorter if a perfect colour match is important.

SHORTENING A ZIP

1 Set your machine to a wide zigzag stitch and adjust the stitch length to 0mm.

2 Stitch about eight to ten zigzag stitches right over the coils where you want the new zip stop to be.

3 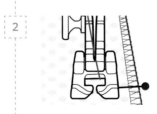 Trim off the thread tails and cut off the excess zip leaving about 2.5cm (1in) below your new zip stop.

YOU WILL NEED:

· Zipper foot
· Seam ripper
· Fabric marker or tailor's chalk
· Pins

CENTRED ZIP

1 Finish your seam allowances by serging, zigzag or pinking; this is extremely hard to do after the zip is installed.

2 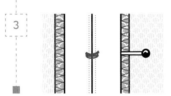 Pin the seam together with right sides facing. Mark where the zip stop goes. Sew the seam together from the mark down to the bottom of the seam.

3  Adjust your stitch length to the longest length and baste the seam together from the top down to your mark. You will eventually be removing these stitches, so do not backstitch. Press the seam open.

SEE ALSO
page 18: Basic feet
page 47: Zips

4 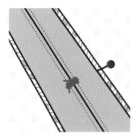 Working on the wrong side, place your zip face down with the zip coil absolutely centred on the seam. Align the zip stop at your mark and pin the zip in place. On the right side, repin and remove the pins from the wrong side.

TIP

Make sure to match the zip colour well as you may end up seeing the zip coils or tape.

5 Install the zipper foot so that the foot is attached on the left half. Adjust your stitch length to standard 2.5mm straight stitch.

6 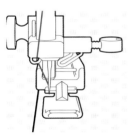 With the seam face up, stitch down the right side of the zip. Line up the left edge of the foot on the seam and use that as your seam guide. Go slow and straight! At the bottom, pivot just before the zip stop and stitch the bottom and backstitch.

7 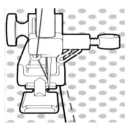 Now move the zipper foot over to the right and stitch down the left side of the zip to the bottom and backstitch.

8 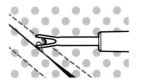 With a seam ripper, carefully rip out the basting stitches and press the seam flat.

SEE ALSO

page 19: Zipper feet
page 116: Seam finishes

YOU WILL NEED:

- Invisible zipper foot
- Regular zipper foot
- Pins

INVISIBLE ZIP

Although the name makes this zip sound intimidating, it is not hard to use since there is not any visible topstitching. So if your stitch is not perfect, who's going to know? The big difference from a regular zip is that with the invisible zip you will install it first and then sew the seam.

1. Finish your seam allowances by serging, zigzag or pinking.

2. Unzip your zip, place it face down on the ironing board and press the coils flat. You will not melt them so do not worry.

3. Install the invisible zipper foot. Make sure that the needle comes down right in the middle of the centre hole.

4. Open your zip and place it face down on the right side of the fabric. Line up the right edge of the zip tape with the edge of the fabric. Slide over so that the coils are exactly 1.6cm (⅝in) from the edge. Pin in place.

5. Line up the zip coil in the LEFT groove of the foot and stitch down until you hit the slider and cannot go any further. Your stitch will be right in the weave that you uncovered when ironing the coils flats.

6

Now lay the other side of the zip face down on the other half of the garment. Make sure the coil is ⅝in (1.6cm) from the edge. Line up the coil into the RIGHT groove and stitch down until you hit the slider.

TIP

If you cannot find the perfect colour match for an invisible zip, go with a darker colour. The darker colour tape will 'hide' more efficiently than a lighter colour. Paint the zip pull with craft paint.

7 Zip up your zip to make sure that no fabric sticks in the coils. If it does, you stitched too close to the coils and you will need to rip out the stitches and re-stitch.

8

Now it is time to finish sewing the seam. Match the seam up right sides together and fold the end of the zip tape over to the right so it does not get caught in the seam. Flatten everything down as much as you can. Install the regular zipper foot on your machine and, starting about 3mm (⅛in) up and 3mm left of the existing seam, sew about 2.5cm (1in).

9

Switch to your all-purpose foot and finish the seam with a 1.6cm (⅝in) seam allowance.

SEE ALSO

page 19: *Zipper feet*
page 116: *Seam finishes*

Glossary of terms

backstitch
Reverse stitches at the beginning and end of a seam used to secure the threads and prevent the seam from coming undone.

basting
A temporary seam using very long stitches. It can also be used to gather fabric by pulling on the bobbin threads. Basting stitches are usually removed when they are no longer needed.

bias grain
The 45-degree angle on fabric between the length and cross grain. Fabrics stretch on the bias.

clip
A small cut into the seam allowance using scissor tips. It is used so seam allowances can spread and lay flat when turned right side out.

cross grain
On a fabric weave, the threads that run from selvage to selvage. Also known as the weft.

dart
A stitched fold of fabric used to shape fabric. Often seen at the waist.

ease
The extra room in a garment to allow for movement and comfort.

edgestitch
Stitching very close – usually 3mm (⅛in) or less – to an edge or seam line.

facing
A piece of fabric sewn to an edge and turned to the inside to conceal seam allowances and finish necklines, armholes and waists.

feed dog
The teeth under the needle plate on a sewing machine that move the fabric.

grainline
Usually refers to the length grain on fabric but also refers to the printed grainline on a pattern.

hem allowance
The total amount of fabric included on a pattern for a hem.

interfacing
A material used to stiffen, strengthen or stabilise another fabric. It can be fused on or sewn in.

length grain
On a fabric weave, the threads that are parallel to the selvage. Also known as the warp.

muslin
A cotton fabric used to make a test garment. Also refers to a test garment itself.

nap
The raised surface on a fabric such as velvet where all the fibres are pointing in one direction. Napped fabrics must be cut as a one-way layout.

one-way print
A print where the design motifs point in one direction. Often seen in prints with animals, buildings, people or words. Must be cut as a one-way layout.

overcast
A seam finishing stitch where the thread wraps over the raw edge.

pinking
A seam finishing technique using pinking shears that make zigzag cuts on the edge to prevent the fabric from fraying.

pivot
A technique to stitch corners where you lower the needle in the fabric, lift the presser foot and turn the fabric around the needle.

raw edge
The unfinished cut edge of a piece of fabric.

right side
The side of fabric that will be visible from the outside of a finished project. Often abbreviated as RS.

seam
A line of stitches that joins two pieces of fabric.

seam allowance
The distance between a seam and the raw edge. Most patterns have seam allowances included and they are usually 1.6cm (⅝in).

seam finish
A technique to prevent the raw edge of a fabric from fraying and raveling. Common seam finishes are pinking, zigzag and serging.

selvage
The finished edges down either side of a length of fabric. They are frequently printed with manufacturer's information and are more tightly woven than the rest of the fabric.

serge
The chain stitch produced by a serger or overlock machine. Can be used as a construction seam or seam finish.

shank
Attaches a presser foot to a sewing machine. Machines are designed for low shank, high shank or slant shank.

slash
To cut into fabric or a pattern to allow it to spread and get larger.

staystitch
A line of stitches used to stabilise an edge and stop it from stretching.

topstitch
Stitching that is usually a 6mm (¼in) from the edge or seam line.

understitch
Stitching the seam allowance to a facing or lining to prevent it from rolling outwards.

warp
On a fabric weave, the threads that are parallel to the selvage. Also known as the length grain.

weft
On a fabric weave, the threads that run from selvage to selvage. Also known as the cross grain.

wrong side
The side of fabric that will not be seen on the outside of a finished project. Often abbreviated as WS.

Resources

ONLINE SUPPLIERS

Bolt
boltfabricboutique.com

Britex
britexfabrics.com

Cool Cottons
coolcottons.biz

Denver Fabrics
denverfabrics.com

Etsy
etsy.com

F & S Fabrics
fandsfabrics.com

Fabric.com
fabric.com

Fashion Fabrics Club
fashionfabricsclub.com

Gorgeous Fabrics
gorgeousfabrics.com

Harts Fabrics
hartsfabric.com

International Silks and Woolens
internationalsilks.com

Liberty
liberty.co.uk

Manhattan Fabrics
manhattanfabrics.com

Michael Levine
mlfabric.com

Mood Fabrics
moodfabrics.com

Paron Fabrics
paronfabrics.com

Robert Kaufman Fabrics
robertkaufman.com

Sew Mama Sew
sewmamasew.com

Stonemountain and
Daughter Fabrics
stonemountainfabric.com

Vogue Fabrics
voguefabricsstore.com/home.php

Westminster Fabrics
Westminsterfabrics.com

WEBSITES AND BLOGS

A Fashionable Stitch
afashionablestitch.com
Authentic handmade style
and fashion

American Sewing Guild
asg.org
A membership organisation for
sewing enthusiasts

Burda Style
burdastyle.com
Projects and patterns for sewers

CRAFT
craftzine.com
Transforming traditional crafts

Collete Patterns Blog
coletterie.com
Sewing tips, ideas and peeks

Gertie's Blog for Better Sewing
blogforbettersewing.com
A homage to Vogue's 1952 better
sewing book

MADE
dana-made-it.com
Includes clothing tutorials

Pattern Review
sewing.patternreview.com
Includes many shop patterns

BOOKS

Chic and Simple Sewing,
by Christine Haynes. Potter
Craft, 2009.

*Claire Shaeffer's Fabric Sewing
Guide,* by Claire Shaeffer. Krause
Publications, 2008.

*Complete Embellishing:
Techniques and Projects,* by Kayte
Terry. Creative Homeowner, 2008.

*Fast Fit Easy Pattern Alterations
for Every Figure,* by Sandra
Betzina. Taunton Press, 2004.

Fit for Real People, by Pati Palmer
and Marta Alto. Palmer-Pletsch
Associates, 2006.

Sew Everything Workshop,
by Diana Rupp. Workman
Publishing, 2007.

Sew U Home Stretch,
by Wendy Mullin. Little Brown
Book Group, 2008.

The New Sewing with a Serger,
Singer Photo Reference Library.
Creative Publishing International,
1999.

*The Vogue/Butterick Step-By-Step
Guide to Sewing Techniques,* by
the editors of Vogue Knitting and
Butterick Patterns Sixth & Spring
Books, 2012.

MAGAZINES

Sew Stylish
craftstylish.com/sewstylish
Includes fashion, restyle
and sewing

Stitch
sewdaily.com/blogs/stitchblog/
pages/about-stitch.aspx
A quarterly sewing magazine
all about creating with fabric
and thread

Threads
threadsmagazine.com
Magazine for sewing enthusiasts,
including garments

Index

Acknowledgements

Thank you so much to all of the people who have taken a sewing class with me over the years. I have learned so much from my students because their questions force me to think of new ways to explain things. Special thanks to Suzan Steinberg of Stonemountain and Daughter Fabrics and Hope Meng, Melissa Rannels and Melissa Alvarado of (the sadly closed) Stitch Lounge for first hiring me to teach sewing classes.

I am always inspired by my crafty friends and their creativity. Thanks to Susan Beal, Cathy Callahan, Linda Permann, Jenny Ryan and Natalie Zee Drieu for asking me to contribute projects and tutorials to your books and magazines.

It was a pleasure to work with the team at RotoVision. Thank you to my editors, Cath Senker and Jane Roe, and to Isheeta Mustafi for hiring me to write this book. Very special thanks to Sherry Heck for her beautiful photographs.

Thank you especially to Vince for being so patient and supportive and always making dinner. This book is dedicated to you.